IN THE WAKE OF DISASTER

IN THE WAKE OF DISASTER

Religious Responses to Terrorism & Catastrophe

Harold G. Koenig, M.D.

TEMPLETON FOUNDATION PRESS

PHILADELPHIA AND LONDON

Templeton Foundation Press
300 Conshohocken State Road, Suite 670
West Conshohocken, PA 19428
www.templetonpress.org

Designed and typeset by Kachergis Book Design

Cover images, left to right: FEMA/Mark Wolfe, FEMA/Andrea
Booher, FEMA/Win Henderson

*Templeton Foundation Press helps intellectual leaders and others
learn about science research on aspects of realities, invisible and
intangible. Spiritual realities include unlimited love, accelerating
creativity, worship, and the benefits of purpose in persons and in
the cosmos.*

Library of Congress Cataloging-in-Publication Data
Koenig, Harold George.
    In the wake of disaster : religious responses to terrorism
and catastrophe
    / Harold G. Koenig.
        p. cm.
    Includes bibliographical references and index.
    ISBN-13: 978-1-932031-99-7 (pbk. : alk. paper)
    ISBN-10: 1-932031-99-5 (pbk. : alk. paper)
    1. Church work with disaster victims—United States.
2. Disasters—Religious aspects.   3. Disasters—Psychological
aspects.   4. Disaster relief—United States.   I. Title.
    HV554.4.K64 2006
    261.8'3—dc22
                                                2005031364

Printed in the United States of America

06   07   08   09   10   10 9 8 7 6 5 4 3 2 1

To the victims of Hurricane Katrina

Contents

Preface

The faith community is often the first to respond to natural disasters and acts of terrorism. Even before Hurricane Katrina made landfall near New Orleans on August 29, 2005, churches were taking in evacuees, and within forty-eight hours after the hurricane hit, they were delivering emergency supplies to victims—well before Federal Emergency Management (FEMA) workers arrived on the scene. This is not an unusual occurrence. In smaller communities, local religious leaders often coordinate the immediate disaster response and later clean up after hurricanes, tornadoes, floods, fire, or acts of terror. Even in larger communities, especially when it comes to providing emotional support, many often turn to the faith community. For example, after September 11, Red Cross workers on the scene in New York City noticed that disaster victims and family members often pushed past clinical psychologists to talk to people with collars on.[1] Disasters and acts of terrorism not only inflict physical damage and loss of life but also leave emotional and spiritual wounds that need healing before victims can rebuild their lives.

In the Wake of Disaster is for people of faith who wish to learn more about disaster preparedness and response, for public policy makers who seek to better prepare their communities for disasters, for emergency response personnel and mental health professionals wanting to know how the faith community can assist them, and for social and behavioral scientists studying the role that religious faith plays in coping with natural disasters and acts of terrorism. Despite the many ways that faith communities can help, their activities often go unrecognized and are seldom integrated into local, regional, or national disaster preparedness and response operations. This book seeks to facilitate that integration by providing information about the unique characteristics and capacities of faith-based organizations and outlining how the formal disaster-response system in the United States works. It is a must-read for those wanting to expand the religious community's role in disaster response and overcome the many barriers and turf battles that now prevent this from happening. The ultimate goal of this book is to increase the resiliency of our communities in the face of disasters by developing the tremendous resources that lie within our faith communities.

Here clergy and faith communities will find information about the psychological, social, and spiritual effects of trauma, the operation of the emergency response system in the United States, and the role that religious faith and faith communities can play in disaster preparation, response, and recovery. The book addresses not only the psychological consequences of disaster but also the spiritual consequences and the effect that spiritual injury may have on the long-term mental health of survivors. It documents the extensive activities of faith communities in meeting the emotional and spiritual needs of disaster victims. It provides practical information on how clergy and faith communities can become better prepared and who to get to know, such as the Red Cross, local emergency management groups, mental health crisis teams, and others.

Federal, state, and local government leaders will find this book a key resource for faith-based responses to disaster that will assist them in developing plans to integrate mental and spiritual care into their emergency management systems (EMS) that respond to natural disasters (hurricanes, floods, earthquakes) or terrorism (explosive events or biological, chemical, nuclear/radiological, cyber attacks, or a combination thereof). Better integration of faith-based efforts with these government services will not only improve the services provided to victims of disasters but also help EMS personnel (firefighters, police, health care providers, etc.) deal better with the emotional and spiritual trauma to which they are exposed so they can remain effective and functional. This will require a system-wide effort to overcome the barriers that faith-based organizations face when responding to disasters. These barriers are described and detailed recommendations to overcome them are given.

Mental health professionals will find useful information on the role of religion and spirituality in coping with disaster stress and trauma. I examine what clergy and faith-based organizations are currently doing to provide mental health care to victims of disaster. The spiritual needs of trauma victims and rescue workers are described and information provided on how mental health providers can assess and address these spiritual needs, and when to refer to trained spiritual caregivers. This information will help to enhance collaboration and cooperation among mental health providers and faith communities and minimize conflict and competition (as so often exists today).

Finally, social and behavioral scientists who study factors that impact emotional and social functioning after disasters and during recovery will find this book a treasure trove of information about studies examining faith-based interventions and their effectiveness, which will assist researchers design future studies in this area.

The information contained here was originally gathered on request of the Center for Mental Health Services (CMHS) of the U.S. Department of Health and Human Services (DHHS). Sources include a comprehensive search of the scientific literature using multiple online databases, a review of the DHHS Mental Health All-Hazards Disaster Planning Guide for state mental health authorities (which in many ways parallels the tasks of faith communities in working together with other disaster-related organizations), and extensive discussions with secular and religious professionals involved in mental health responses to local and national disasters. The result is a relatively concise and yet comprehensive guide for appreciating and integrating faith-based resources into local, state, and national efforts to help our communities deal with the immediate and long-term consequences of natural disasters and acts of terrorism.

Acknowledgments

This book would not have been possible without the help of Joanna Hill and Laura Barrett of Templeton Foundation Press and disaster experts Francis Gunn,[1] Zahara Davidowitz-Farkas,[2] Johanna Olson,[3] and David Pollock.[4]

The Center for Mental Health Studies, Substance Abuse and Mental Health Services Administration, U.S. Department of Health and Human Services, provided partial support for this project; a special thanks to Captain John Tuskan and others at the Center for Mental Health Studies.

Introduction

Each year millions of residents of the United States incur injuries or property damage that result from disasters, costing as much as $1 billion a week.[1,2] This does not include cataclysmic events such as Hurricane Katrina, which may eventually cost over $200 billion[3] and has taken over one thousand lives.[4] While this book focuses on disasters in the United States, the reader should not lose sight of disasters happening regularly all over the world of much greater scope than any that have ever touched this country—from the December 26, 2004, tsunami in the Indian Ocean that killed 275,000 people[5] to an October 8, 2005, earthquake that killed 83,000,[6] injured 75,000,[7] and left 4 million homeless[8] in Pakistan.

Faith-based and community organizations (FBOs) serve a critical role in the immediate and long-term response to natural disasters, unintended human-caused disasters, and intentional acts of terrorism. That role, however, has yet to be clearly described or fully comprehended.

Although occasionally referred to in off-handed ways, faith-based organizations have received little attention from government and emergency management agencies, and little sustained effort has been made to integrate their activities into formal disaster preparedness and response systems. The potential role of FBOs became evident when the United States was stunned by the 9/11 terrorist attacks on the World Trade Center and Pentagon. A national survey of the U.S. population published in the *New England Journal of Medicine* one week later reported that nine out of ten Americans turned to religion in order to cope with the fear and uncertainty that these events caused.[9] A national poll sponsored by the Red Cross after 9/11 reported that 60 percent of respondents said they would be more likely to seek help from a spiritual caregiver than either a physician (45%) or a mental health professional (40%).[10]

During the first few days after Hurricane Katrina, while FEMA and other government agencies were organizing their response, religious organizations provided immediate assistance to victims.[11] Before the storm hit, evacuees found housing, supplies, and fellowship in churches that opened their doors to them. Immediately afterward, many local religious organizations, as well as those in surrounding states (as far north as Michigan) served as emergency shelters providing refuge for hurricane victims. One church in Baton Rouge fed sixteen thousand people daily during the week after the storm. Other churches from all over the country collected donations of money and supplies such as paper goods, clothing, food, and school supplies, and organized teams of volunteers who traveled to the Gulf Coast to distribute them. One of these churches sent eighteen semi-truck trailers worth of supplies to shelters and other agencies during the first week. As time passed after Katrina, religious organizations continued to provide services ranging from neighborhood cleanup activities to building showers, helping victims find jobs, even providing free haircuts.

The widespread lack of recognition and appreciation for the faith community's role in disaster response is surprising given that Quakers, Mennonites, and the Salvation Army have been involved in helping disaster victims for over fifty years, and almost every major religious denomination in the United States has participated in disaster relief during the past fifteen to thirty years.

Why do faith communities play such an important role? Disaster expert Francis Gunn gives ten reasons:

1. Faith traditions and local faith communities are considered a primary means of spiritual and social support.

2. Faith traditions often include rituals, worship, and prayers that are viewed as a means for accessing divine intervention, divine power, protection, and healing in times of threat or trouble.

3. The very presence of a faith tradition in the community, often symbolized by a church, synagogue, mosque, etc., testifies to beliefs that have endured the test of time, causing these institutions to be viewed as "cornerstones" of a community.

4. Most faith traditions preach or teach a message that can serve as a source of strength to calm peoples' fears and fortify peoples' belief and hope. This message is sometimes communicated through parables or stories that have endured for generations and may be easily accessed because they live on in the consciousness of believers.

5. Religious leaders such as priests, ministers, rabbis, and imams may be automatically associated with "God coming to our aid." They are often viewed as providing reassurance, the promise of divine help, and a comforting, healing presence.

6. Most faith communities train their clergy to assist people in times of loss and tragedy and many clergy have considerable experience with supporting people through these difficult times.

7. Faith communities have a tradition of coming to the aid of their fellow believers. This provides a natural source of assistance in meeting physical, emotional, and spiritual needs. It also gives people the powerful message, "You are not alone in this; we will be with you."

8. After other "emergency services" have served their purpose and are withdrawn from a community, people know that their faith communities will remain there to be an ongoing source of support.

9. People who might be wary or hesitant to seek mental health support or services might still be willing to turn to their faith community for similar types of support since there is no "stigma" attached to such help.

10. Many faith traditions have regional, national, or even global networks that can help to provide assistance, financial and otherwise, to a local faith community. When it comes to gathering monetary resources, most faith traditions are trusted organizations to which people will feel comfortable contributing. Thus, they are good resources for helping fund disaster assistance.

I'd like to add that with the Internet religious organizations have a way of obtaining online financial donations that can be immediately used for helping victims. Legal barriers and chains of approval that slow government agencies from providing such resources do not stand in the way of religious organizations, which can make these funds available almost instantly.

Overview

Because of the tremendous role that faith communities play in responding to disasters, especially in addressing psychological and spiritual needs, that role needs to be carefully examined, its scope and value more fully appreciated, and ways to expand and support such activities more completely explored, which are the purposes of this book. I briefly summarize each chapter below.

Chapter 1 examines the psychological and spiritual responses to disaster, emphasizing the psychological stages that victims go through after the initial trauma. Understanding normal responses to trauma will help faith communities know when their help is needed most and what kind of help is needed at different points in time. The impact that disaster has on religious faith is also explored, since injuries to spiritual worldviews may underlie long-term negative psychological reactions to trauma.

Chapter 2 discusses national, state, and local emergency management systems (EMS) that become active when disaster strikes. More fully, understanding the existing EMS will help faith communities see where their efforts can be most effective. Gaps in the formal emergency response system are highlighted, especially in terms of providing psychological and spiritual care over time.

Chapter 3 explores the role that religion plays in coping with stress in general and then reviews research on how religion has helped victims of disasters in particular. The chapter also examines how religion helps people heal psychologically and move on with their lives after severe trauma and loss, and discusses how religion may strengthen them to deal with future life traumas.

Chapter 4 moves from religion as a personal coping resource to religion as a force that motivates people of faith to help victims of disaster. Here I review studies that describe the role of clergy and lay volunteers in responding to natural and manmade disasters. A palpable religious presence has characterized virtually every major disaster in U.S. history, and may be one of the major reasons why our communities have bounced back as quickly as they have.

Chapter 5 describes faith-based organizations that have in recent years been involved in disasters, focusing on special units within these organizations that are mobilized whenever and wherever disaster strikes. Virtually every major religious group has such a response team, and these teams are described. I also examine organizations that have developed in order to coordinate volunteer and faith-based efforts during disasters. Such organizations came about because of a fragmented and disorganized faith response in the past that wasted resources and even impeded relief efforts in some instances.

Chapter 6 provides details on how faith-based efforts can be coordinated at the local level, depending on the size of the community affected. Also discussed are suggestions by disaster experts on who should lead such efforts in order to maximize the contributions of spiritually motivated individuals and religious communities.

Chapter 7 focuses on how faith communities can get ready for such events, and thus be the givers of help rather than the victims. For faith communities to have their maximum impact, they must be sufficiently organized and informed prior to disasters so that they can immediately mobilize resources. I review a disaster plan on how faith communities can ready themselves to ensure the survival of their own members as well as meet the needs of others in the community who may be affected.

Chapter 8 examines barriers and obstacles that stand in the way of faith communities being more fully integrated into the formal disaster response system. Lack of information on how to respond, territoriality and competition, lack of cooperation and coordination, and differences in theology can prevent religious volunteers and organizations from becoming a central part of our nation's response to disasters.

Chapter 9 examines ways to overcome these barriers through research, education, leadership, and changes in attitude. Based on suggestions by disaster experts, I make specific recommendations that EMS agencies, public policy makers, mental health organizations, and faith communities can implement in order to address barriers to integration.

Chapter 10 makes observations about the relevance of this topic to faith communities, government agencies, and mental health professionals, and emphasizes the future impact that individuals and communities of faith can have in helping communities not only bounce back after disasters but also become stronger and more resilient as a result.

A section on resources provides information on Web sites, organizations, books, pamphlets, and published research that will help the reader obtain more in-depth knowledge about the role of FBOs in responding to disasters.

This volume represents the most detailed examination to date of what faith communities can contribute to our response to natural disasters and acts of terrorism. While we will always heavily rely on the formal EMS system to respond to the immediate needs of disaster victims, that system alone is not sufficient. The short-term and long-term psychological and spiritual needs of victims are simply too great. Those needs require a healing community that understands and, over time, supports and loves them back to health and wholeness.

IN THE WAKE OF DISASTER

one

Psychological and Spiritual Consequences of Disasters

In order to prepare to meet the psychological and spiritual needs of disaster victims in a timely and sensitive manner, members of the faith community, mental health counselors, and EMS workers must be aware of what those needs are. This chapter describes the typical psychological and spiritual reactions following disasters, emphasizing *when* such reactions occur during the course of disaster and its aftermath. The timing of interventions is crucial if they are to be effective.

Psychological Reactions

There are distinct time periods or phases at the onset of the disaster that are associated with typical psychological reactions. Those psychological reactions will vary depending on the type of disaster or trauma; on its severity, scope, and geographical location; and on the personality and mental health of the victim. However, consistent patterns have been observed.

The time periods following a disaster can be divided into the (1) impact phase, (2) early aftermath phase, (3) short-term aftermath phase, and (4) long-term aftermath phase.[1] The psychological reactions associated with each of these phases may occur in a different order depending on the particular person and, in some cases, stages may be prolonged or shortened. Nevertheless, understanding these phases will help to determine when assistance from the faith community is most needed and when victims are likely to be most receptive.

Impact Phase

This is the period that begins immediately after the onset of a disaster and continues until the physical damage is completed. During this time, most people experience hyperarousal or alertness, feel varying degrees of fear, and may experience shock or a sense of numbness. Although some may become immobilized or experience panic and attempt to flee from the scene, most individuals will behave rationally and constructively by seeking information and resources to help them cope with the event.[2] Emotional responses will depend heavily on the intrapsychic and social resources that the person has immediately available. Any factor, however, that increases a feeling of personal control over the event or conveys a sense of being looked after or watched over will help to reduce the overall impact of the trauma.[3]

Early Aftermath Phase

Sometimes called the crisis phase, this period begins immediately following the disaster, when rescue teams and emergency workers are focused on providing physical care, helping the injured, and preserving property. This is often a time characterized by chaos, especially when no disaster planning has taken place. The psychosocial needs of persons during this phase are often ignored; the priority is on physical needs. Psychological reactions among survivors include high levels of anxiety, heightened physiological responses (trembling, heart and blood pressure changes, gastrointestinal or genitourinary symptoms), and acute grief over loss.

Psychological needs at this time are best met by explanation (information giving), reassurance, and instruction. Efforts to get these individuals to talk about their feelings when they are "just trying to find out what happened to their families, children, or their homes," however, is not very helpful.[4] Simply offering companionship and a caring presence may be best at this stage.

Short-Term Aftermath Phase

This is also called the "processing" phase, as rescue workers begin to withdraw from the scene and people begin to recognize the implications of the disaster event and their need for support. By four weeks after Hurricane Katrina, the news media began reporting on the emergence of sleeplessness, anxiety, domestic violence, and despair.[5] "It's as if you're carrying an extra twenty pounds on your shoulders," one victim reported. "The emotional fatigue has just worn everyone out."

During this phase, psychosocial interventions are most important and victims are most receptive. It is now that people begin to grieve over the losses that they have experienced and may actively seek out others for support. There is often need to attribute "meaning" to the disaster event. Meaning helps people to psychologically integrate traumatic experiences into their existing worldviews. People need time to work through their losses in a "safe place" and arrive at a coherent and satisfactory explanation for the event. Even if this explanation is a negative one (God's judgment for sin, for example), having a bad explanation is still better than having no explanation at all. Much caution, then, should be taken before simply dismissing such explanations, since the person may be using them to hold his or her world together. People also need time to periodically escape from grieving and attend to other practical needs; thus, it is important to follow cues from the victim as to how much support he or she needs at any particular moment.

Long-Term Aftermath Phase

This period begins at a time when most victims have more or less psychologically integrated the traumatic event (6–12 months afterward). However, such integration may last for the rest of a person's life as he or she slowly and more fully adapts to the changes and losses that have occurred. Psychosocial support may be gradually tapered off during this time. This phase can also be associated with a "let down" feeling for both helpers and victims. Rituals, memorials, and commemorative events to honor the incident become important (i.e., yearly anniversaries). Although most individuals proceed with adaptation, some may continue to experience emotional distress and remain impaired. Still others may have delayed grief reactions during this time. Continued or periodic social, psychological, and spiritual support may be necessary for years.

These are the usual stages that disaster victims pass through. For disasters like Hurricane Katrina, however, the stages of psychological response and adaptation may not follow the usual pattern. With Katrina there were multiple waves of disaster. First there was the hurricane and its destruction, then came the flooding, then the forced relocation, then the botched relief efforts with its complications, and finally the prolonged displacement of people away from friends and family. In such circumstances, what we learned about treating survivors of discrete events like September 11 or the Oklahoma City bombing may not apply. Over the long term, experts are saying that Post-Traumatic Stress Disorder may be much more of a serious problem after a disaster like Katrina than after disasters this country faced previously.[6]

Long-Term Psychological Consequences

Long-term adverse psychological consequences are common following natural disasters and terrorist acts. An analysis of fifty-two disaster studies revealed that the most common psychological problems are anxiety (40%), physical complaints (36%), alcohol use (36%), phobia (fear of a specific object or situation) (32%), and depression (26%).[7] Nearly 90 percent of the U.S. population has been through at least one event that traumatized them psychologically, and between 8 percent and 15 percent have developed the full syndrome of Post-Traumatic Stress Disorder (PTSD), with many others experiencing Acute Stress Disorder (ASD).[8,9] Some experts report that 50 to 80 percent of those surviving severe disasters may develop PTSD symptoms.[10] Disasters can lead to PTSD or ASD in both survivors and rescue workers.

As indicated above, psychological reactions may be specific to the type of event that occurs, whether a natural disaster or an act of terrorism or war.

Natural Disasters

About 30 percent of persons directly affected by natural disasters develop PTSD.[11] For example, when survivors were surveyed six to twelve months after Hurricane Andrew swept through South Florida in 1992, the prevalence of PTSD was 36 percent, major depression was 30 percent, generalized anxiety disorder was 11 percent, and panic disorder was 10 percent.[12] In 1972, a dam collapsed in Buffalo Creek, West Virginia, resulting in 250 deaths. Following the event, nearly 60 percent of those affected had symptoms of PTSD and 28 percent continued to have PTSD for at least fourteen years (30% continued to have other psychopathology as well).[13,14] Thus, while the traumatic psychological effects of natural disasters can be short-lived, they can often last for years.[15]

Acts of Terrorism

Studies in the United States are less common with regard to human-caused disasters or acts of terrorism. The two events for which there is the most information are the Oklahoma City bombing and the September 11 World Trade Center attacks. A survey conducted six months after the 1995 Oklahoma City bombing found that 34 percent of survivors had PTSD, 74 percent of which were new cases.[16] Also in that study, television exposure was correlated with post-traumatic stress symptoms in middle school students seven weeks after the event. Similarly, in a survey of 1,008 adults conducted five to eight weeks after the September 11, rates of PTSD reached 8 percent and rates of depression 10 percent in the Manhattan area overall.[17] However, PTSD rates increased to 20 percent among persons who lived near the World Trade Center. In Israel, after three years of escalating war and terrorism (2001–2004), 314 participants from three communities were surveyed (Tel-Aviv, Kiryat-Arba, and Gush-Katif settlements).[18] Acute stress and PTSD symptoms ranged from 60.7 percent to 85.4 percent, with the lowest rates in the Gush-Katif Settlements (Gaza Strip) and the highest near Tel-Aviv.

Combat and War

With regard to PTSD during wartime, nearly 15 percent of those seeing action in Vietnam developed the disorder.[19] Rates of psychological trauma have been similar for soldiers returning from the more recent war in the Middle East. A study of 3,671 U.S. infantry troops three to four months after their return from combat found that that 15.6 percent to 17.1 percent of those returning from Iraq and 11.2 percent of those returning from Afghanistan met criteria for major depression, generalized anxiety, or PTSD.[20]

Those at Greatest Risk

Who is most vulnerable to negative psychological reactions after disasters? Surprisingly, the adult group most affected by the stress of natural disasters is middle-aged Americans (ages 31 to 65), because of their multiple responsibilities and roles.[21] Children, however, can also be affected. Following Hurricane Hugo (1989) in South Carolina, 5 percent of school-aged children met criteria for PTSD at three months after the event, with girls and younger children at greater risk.[22] EMS workers are another high-risk group. One study of firefighters involved in battling brushfires found that 69 percent of those who had stress reactions four months following the fires continued to experience symptoms nearly 2½ years after the event.[23] In general, about 16 percent of firefighters experience PTSD at some point during their lives.[24]

The strongest predictor of PTSD risk is proximity to the trauma and intensity of exposure.[25] Risk is also greater when the trauma is intentionally inflicted by another person, as in rape, crime, or acts of terrorism. Following the World Trade Center (WTC) attacks on September 11, persons most affected were Hispanics, those having two or more prior stressors, those experiencing a panic attack shortly after the events, those living close to the WTC towers, and those who lost possessions because of the attacks.[26] Those at greatest risk for *depression* following the WTC attacks were again Hispanics, those having two or more prior stressors, and those experiencing a panic attack soon after the events. Additional risk factors for depression included a low level of social support, death of a friend or relative, and loss of a job due to the attacks.

Other predictors of poor psychological outcome following disasters include female gender, lower education, and lower social class. Prior psychopathology (major depression or anxiety disorder) may lead to greater susceptibility, although this is not yet proven.[27,28] Firstborn or only children experience more fear and anxiety following a storm, flood, or earthquake.[29] Locus of control is a psychological factor consistently related to negative reactions following disasters. Persons who retained a belief in a world in which they can control outcomes (i.e., those with an internal locus of control) cope better with disasters.[30] Inadequate social support can also increase the risk of PTSD.[31]

Having a belief system that confers a sense of control or involvement in a supportive community with common beliefs committed to helping one another, could also impact PTSD risk following disasters.

A Pastoral Perspective

Pastoral counselor and disaster expert Francis Gunn describes the impact that trauma and disaster has on the victim.[32] The points he makes here reinforce and expand upon those made above.

Since the beginning of human belief in a Supreme Being or some kind of Divine reality, people have sought comfort and strength from their religious beliefs. This is especially true in times of great difficulty, struggle, or suffering. Religious beliefs express, in part, a person or community's faith in the enduring presence of a divine being or beings who can be turned to for healing and meaning in difficult times. Traumatic experiences are generally defined as events or circumstances that are outside the realm of ordinary experience which break through one's defenses in such a way that they overwhelm one's ability to cope or function. The scope of the incident or traumatic experience will affect the nature of the impact and the ability of a person or community to cope and or resume normal functioning. Some factors which affect the severity of the impact are:

1) The nature of the incident and/or the severity of the threat

2) The duration of the event

3) The level of exposure to the threat

4) The level of pre-incident equilibrium in the life of a person or the experience of a community

5) The degree to which there was some warning or ability to prepare for the traumatic event

There are various phases or stages to traumatic experiences or community disasters which also impact how people cope. The initial response to a traumatic event or disaster is focused on re-establishing order and a sense of safety/security. During this time emergency service professionals often take charge and there may be considerable effort focused on the rescue and treatment of victims and the assessment of damage or loss. This may be called the "rescue stage," and can last minutes, days, or weeks. During this time people will focus on finding and rescuing loved ones who may be unaccounted for.

There comes a point where the rescue operation shifts to what can be called the "recovery stage," not to be confused with the process of emotional and spiritual recovery. During this time rescue agencies will re-orient their strategies toward the recovery of the dead and cleanup of the site or sites. With each passing day the possibility of finding survivors dwindles until a point is reached where there is little possibility of finding anyone alive. This can be an especially difficult time for surviving loved ones since they have been holding out hope for the extraordinary rescue or the so-called "miracle" followed by the overwhelming relief and euphoria of discovering that loved one(s) are alive and out of harm's way. As the dead are identified and the scope of the tragedy are assessed the person or community may begin to regain some sense of control and be able to deal with the consequences of what has happened. During this time acceptance of the reality of the tragedy and coping often begin with memorial and prayer services for families and communities. After deceased loved ones are memorialized people begin the process of attempting to return to their routines, yet there are all kinds of factors that can complicate this phase of adjustment. These include:

1) A recovery stage of long duration where the remains of loved ones are not found or identified for weeks, months, or perhaps not at all. This may lead to many questions about how to ritual or memorialize a loss.

2) The media coverage of the event can contribute to a kind of re-traumatization through continual re-exposure to the images and stories surrounding a disaster.

3) The procurement of monetary compensation and reimbursements and the complexities can be a cause of ongoing stress and threat. This is especially true if people believe that their needs are not being addressed justly or expeditiously.

4) Any process of civil or criminal litigation, court cases, etc., can keep an event and its consequences before the eyes of individuals, families, and communities for undetermined periods of time.

5) Establishing responsibility or negligence related to the causes of a traumatic event or disaster can provoke intense emotional responses in people and communities.

6) Decisions about permanent memorials after community disasters can also contribute to ongoing tension and stress.

7) Several of the above can lead to ongoing tensions and divisions in families or communities that threaten to erode or destroy previous bonds and support systems. This is in itself can develop into a kind of traumatic loss.

The scope of disasters, the nature of their impact, and the various phases of coping and adjustment are directly related to how people and communities utilize their spiritual resources and beliefs to cope, find strength, discover meaning, and ultimately heal from the wounds of trauma and loss.

Loss of Faith

Although religious or spiritual beliefs may represent a profound source of comfort, meaning, and hope following disasters for many people, sometimes it is a person's faith that is the victim. The kind of emotional trauma that might be experienced by persons living through a disaster where limbs are lost or loved ones are killed or severely injured impacts not only a person's sense of self and social relationships but also his or her faith and belief in God.[33]

According to Janoff-Bulman, severe traumatic stress shatters victims' basic assumptions about themselves and their world, including what they believe.[34] Faith involves that which gives order and meaning to life, and is based on a number of assumptions that can be radically challenged by living through a disaster. Such an experience can dramatically affect belief in a universe that is ordered and controlled by a loving God. This may plunge the person into a state of existential crisis and spiritual disarray. A person's *basic sense of trust*, which is crucial for faith and for psychological stability,[35] can be altered by the traumatic experience. Herman describes what this is like:

> In situations of terror people spontaneously. . . cry . . . for God. When this cry is not answered, the basic sense of trust is shattered. Traumatized people feel utterly abandoned, utterly alone, cast out of the human and divine systems of care and protection that sustain life. Therefore, a sense of alienation, a disconnection, pervades every relationship, from the most intimate familial bonds to the most abstract affiliations of community and religion.[36]

Wilson and Moran also emphasize this point:

> Following massively traumatic events, one becomes acutely aware that "bad things" can and do happen despite a deep and enduring sense of faith, trust, and belief in the Divine. Once that inner sense of trust which sustained faith is disrupted and compromised, the individual feels betrayed (by long-held beliefs), disillusioned, and disconnected. Oftentimes the traumatized person feels abandoned and destined to a spiritual life of hopelessness and gloom. In its acute state, this spiritual malaise leaves the traumatized individual feeling isolated, estranged, and alienated from self, the community of faith, and from God.[37]

That sense of abandonment is common among severely traumatized individuals. Even Jesus, toward the end of his crucifixion, called out with his last breath—"My God, my God, why hast thou forsaken me?"[38] This is a universal feeling, and prompts such questions as "Why me"? "How could God allow this to happen?" "Has God abandoned me?" "Is God punishing me?" And finally, "Does God even exist?" This may result in a decline in spirituality and, in some instances, a complete loss of faith. There is some evidence that when people become "stuck" here questioning God's love for them and power to make a difference, even their physical health may be adversely affected.[39]

Victims of disaster often experience an intense search for meaning and purpose in life, having lost their footing in a previous faith system. For this reason, it is crucial to be sensitive to the spiritual needs (especially spiritual injuries) of victims as a result of the trauma and to direct those persons to pastoral counselors trained to address these issues. Otherwise, a spiritually traumatized person can become hardened and numb—without faith, trust, or hope.[40] Because intact religious beliefs can help facilitate recovery from severe trauma,[41] especially over the long term,[42,43] when this resource is no longer available, the risk of long-term mental health problems may increase.

A recent study of 1,385 veterans from Vietnam (95%), World War II, and/or Korea (5%) being treated in outpatient or inpatient PTSD programs documented the impact that spiritual injury can have on mental health.[44] Alan Fontana and Robert Rosenheck, from the VA National Center for PTSD and Yale University School of Medicine, examined the interrelationships between veterans' exposure to traumatic stress, PTSD, change in religious faith, and use of mental health services. They used a sophisticated statistical analysis called structural equation modeling to show that veterans' traumatic experiences during war often weakened their religious faith (i.e., caused a spiritual injury). Weakened religious faith, in turn, was one of the most powerful predictors of use of VA mental health services—regardless of severity of PTSD symptoms or level of social functioning. The need for mental health services, then, was driven more by previously unrecognized spiritual injury than by clinical symptoms or social factors. Investigators concluded that pastoral counseling to address spiritual injury should become a central part of the treatment of PTSD patients.

In other cases, individuals who experience stressful trauma may actually become stronger. This change, called "stress-related growth,"[45] is the result of psychological and spiritual maturing that occurs when a person successfully deals with a stressor. Such a person may be more resilient when facing future difficulties. Religious involvement has been shown to predict greater stress-related growth among stressed populations.[46,47]

Pastors and pastoral counselors need to provide trauma victims with the kind of spiritual resources that will enable psychological and spiritual growth to take place. Addressing spiritual needs can help victims emerge from these circumstances as more mature, better human beings—rather than as wounded individuals struggling for years or decades from psychological and/or spiritual traumas that have not been adequately addressed.

Including the spiritual component, then, may help not only those with PTSD but also the many more persons who experience lower levels of poor mental health or psychological wounds that detract from quality of life. Reestablishing a sense of order, meaning, and safety by helping persons to utilize spiritual resources may contribute to the healing of such wounds, whether small or large.

Summary

Many people experience serious problems with anxiety and depression following disasters. This chapter describes and underscores the social, psychosocial, and spiritual needs that often go unmet after these events. Psychological trauma may persist long after the immediate post-disaster period, often lasting many months or years. Local faith communities are often left to pick up the pieces and try to help people put their lives back together, a role that is often ignored by emergency response agencies concerned with immediate physical needs and short-term psychological needs. Disaster trauma also affects people's faith and spiritual belief systems. Because of the potential long-term consequences of spiritual injuries on mental health, spiritual care following disaster may be important. All disaster victims should be screened for unmet psychological and spiritual needs and referred to trained spiritual caregivers (and mental health professionals) as necessary. For some, long-term recovery may depend first on spiritual healing.

Effective disaster response requires identifying factors related to psychological resiliency and resources contained within communities that help minimize mental health consequences. Religious faith and the availability of trained clergy and lay volunteers may be among those factors and resources. Before discussing the impact of faith in coping with disaster and the role that clergy and faith communities can and do play in this process, I will examine the structures and organization of the formal disaster response system in the United States today.

two

National, State, and Local Disaster Planning and Response

To determine where clergy and faith communities fit into overall disaster planning and response, it is necessary to understand the current activities of national, state, and local groups that form the formal disaster and emergency response system. These groups are described below with an emphasis on their primary functions and whether or not they include addressing emotional or spiritual needs.

National Organizations

Federal Emergency Management Agency (FEMA)

Because of a serious lack of coordination of agencies involved in disaster relief, federal legislation (1974 Robert T. Stafford Disaster Relief and Emergency Assistance Act) was passed to address this problem and provide financial assistance during times of disaster. This includes funding to address the mental health needs of disaster victims (Crisis Counseling Program). The Disaster Relief Act led to the establishment of FEMA in 1979. However, FEMA traces its beginnings to the Congressional Act of 1803, which provided assistance to a town in New Hampshire after a fire nearly destroyed it. Since then, Congress has passed legislation to deal with hurricanes, floods, fires, earthquakes, and other disasters over one hundred times.

Formerly an independent agency, FEMA joined twenty-two other federal agencies in March 2003 as part of the new Department of Homeland Security (DHS).[1] This new department (DHS) was designed to coordinate the nation's approach to national security, including natural disasters or terrorist attacks, and has received billions of dollars to accomplish this purpose. FEMA is one of four major branches of this department. FEMA's headquarters is located in Washington, D.C., and has ten regional offices and two area offices, including the Mount Weather Emergency Operations Center and the FEMA training center in Emmitsburg, Maryland. FEMA has more than 2,500 full-time employees and nearly 5,000 standby disaster assistance employees who move into action when disasters occur. FEMA works in partnership with several other organizations that are part of the nation's emergency response system, including state and local emergency agencies, nearly thirty other federal agencies, and the American Red Cross. Since Hurricane Katrina, several senators have introduced bills in Congress that would make FEMA an independent agency once again.[2,3]

What Does FEMA Do?   When the president declares a disaster, he appoints a Federal Coordinating Officer (FCO) for each state affected by the disaster. The FCO, along with the state response team, sets up a Disaster Field Office near the disaster. FEMA, however, does a lot more than coordinate the federal government's response to disasters. It advises on building codes and flood plain management; provides public education on disasters; equips local and state EMS agencies for disaster planning; distributes disaster financial assistance to states, communities, businesses, and individuals; trains EMS personnel; supports local firefighters; and administers national flood and crime insurance programs. The functions of FEMA can be divided into six areas: *prepare* for disasters, *respond* to disasters, facilitate *recovery* from disasters, *mitigate* the effects of disasters, *reduce the risk of loss*, and *prevent* disasters from occurring in the first place. I will briefly describe each of these functions.

Prepare. Preparedness involves figuring out what to do if essential services break down, developing a plan for responding to such a breakdown, and practicing the plan—that is, planning, training, and exercising. With regard to planning, FEMA funds EMS programs and personnel in every state. States each have an Emergency Operation Plan that is updated periodically and submitted to FEMA for review to ensure that it is current. With regard to training, FEMA's training center in Emmitsburg includes the

Emergency Management Institute and the National Fire Academy. Emergency managers, firefighters, and elected officials in states and local municipalities can travel there to take classes on emergency management. Classes include emergency planning, design and evaluation of disaster management, hazardous materials response, and fire service management. These FEMA courses are sometimes given regionally by states to local EMS personnel. Finally, for private citizens who want to know more about these areas, an Independent Study Program is available at the FEMA website.[4]

Respond. When a disaster occurs, emergency equipment must be brought into the field, people need to be gotten out of danger's path, and basic supplies such as food, water, and shelter must be provided to survivors. Medical services may also be needed. Damaged services need to be repaired and gotten back into operation (phone, electricity, natural gas, sewer, water). The first to respond are local personnel such as police, firemen, and sometimes non-injured citizens. It is not until the destruction goes beyond the ability of local and state EMS agencies to contain it that FEMA becomes involved. At that time, state and local governments can make a request for federal aid through a presidential disaster declaration. The kind of federal aide usually provided is financial, although FEMA has the authority to mobilize resources from other federal agencies as part of the Federal Response Plan.

Recovery. FEMA also helps people and communities rebuild after the disaster is over. This process of returning to normal can take a long time. Recovery includes reestablishing services and infrastructure, rebuilding facilities, reorganizing operations, and helping people put their lives back together, including coping with lost loved ones, possessions, and jobs. FEMA offers loans and grants that can help rebuild homes or businesses, rebuild public facilities, clear debris, repair roads, and restore water, sewer, electricity, and other local services.

Mitigate. Mitigation seeks to lessen the impact of disasters by such measures as ensuring building safely within a floodplain, removing homes that are in danger, ensuring that buildings and infrastructures are built to withstand earthquakes. By creating and enforcing building codes, FEMA minimizes the impact of floods, hurricanes, and other natural hazards by addressing foreseeable problems before they occur.

Risk Reduction. An example of risk reduction is protection against the damage caused by floods. The major way that FEMA reduces the cost of floods is by the Federal Insurance Administration (FIA). The FIA collaborates with national insurance companies to provide affordable flood insurance. By complying with FEMA floodplain regulations, communities become eligible for such insurance. Thus, not only is insurance available for unavoidable damage but the risk of damage is lessened as communities comply with floodplain building safety.

Prevention. FEMA makes every effort to prevent emergencies and disasters when possible. Again, by establishing codes and regulations, effort is made to prevent chemical explosions, hazardous materials spills, and fires. The United States Fire Administration (USFA) educates the public on measures to prevent fires, including installing smoke detectors, using space heaters safely, not smoking in hazardous areas, and so forth.

In summary, through its education efforts, FEMA seeks to prepare community emergency systems to respond to disasters. Through various federal, state, and local regulations and laws, FEMA attempts to minimize the damage and loss that disasters are likely to have. By providing insurance and direct financial assistance to survivors and affected communities, FEMA helps to lessen the impact of disasters after everything has been done to minimize that impact through planning and prevention activities.

Red Cross

The Red Cross was started when Henry Dunant organized local citizens to take care of dead and wounded soldiers during a battle between Austria and Sardinia in 1859. The volunteers bandaged soldiers' wounds, fed them, and provided them with kindness and support. Later, Dunant worked to create national relief societies to assist those wounded in battle (which eventually led to the Geneva Conventions). In 1863, the International Red Cross and Red Crescent movement developed in Switzerland out of these relief societies with the goal of providing nonpartisan care to the wounded and sick during times of war. The Red Cross movement today includes the Geneva-based International Committee of the Red Cross (ICRC), the International Federation of Red Cross and Red Crescent Societies, and national societies located in 175 countries, including the American Red Cross in the United States.[5]

Because it is not a governmental agency, the Red Cross operates largely on charitable donations and the work of volunteers. The American Red Cross Disaster Relief Fund enables the Red Cross to provide shelter, food, counseling, and other assistance to those in need. The usual method of donating to the Red Cross is either to contribute money directly to the Relief Fund or to purchase vouchers for the survivors that they can redeem at local stores. This process also helps to channel money into the local economy and thus aids the community in recovery from disaster. Large corporations may donate food, bottled water, and other items needed by disaster-affected communities, although donations of this sort from individuals are not usually accepted.

The Red Cross is not a religious organization or religiously affiliated, and its symbol, the red cross, is not considered a religious symbol, although it is used primarily in Christian countries. The red cross is replaced with the "red crescent" in most Islamic countries and by the "red shield of David" in Israel.

What Does the American Red Cross Do? The primary mission of the American Red Cross, which sees itself as "a humanitarian organization led by volunteers," is to provide relief to victims of disasters and help people prevent, prepare for, and respond to emergencies wherever they occur in the United States or where Americans live or fight around the world. The American Red Cross is not part of the U.S. Government, but works closely with organizations such as FEMA and with the U.S. Armed Forces. During war, the American Red Cross operates by a charter that enables it to remain impartial and neutral, as with the International Red Cross.

According to its Web site, the American Red Cross provides half the nation's blood supply and blood products. It also provides health and safety training to the public and provides emergency social services to members of the U.S. military and their families. Red Cross staff live and work in the same dangerous environments as U.S. troops. Their tasks include giving comfort to soldiers by providing emergency messages about deaths and births, comfort kits, and blank cards to send letters home to loved ones.

In the wake of an earthquake, tornado, flood, fire, hurricane, or other disaster, the Red Cross is often among the first organizations that appear on the scene to provide relief. An example of the Red Cross in action was the terrorist attack of September 11, 2001, which cost the Red Cross nearly $1 billion in disaster aid. This event involved the largest mobilization of volunteers for a disaster relief operation in U.S. history, with 54,577 volunteers and workers providing relief at the scene. Response to Hurricane Katrina no doubt has far surpassed these figures.

The Red Cross also provides guidance on the most effective way that individuals can contribute to relief efforts during times of disaster, especially with regard to in-kind contributions (which the Red Cross itself does not accept). American Red Cross website has specific instructions on how individuals and businesses can best help during disasters.[6]

National Voluntary Organizations
Active in Disasters (NVOAD)

For many years, small and large voluntary organizations served disaster victims largely independent of one another. This resulted in duplication of services and excess help in some disaster locations and absence of services in other locations. Volunteers were often frustrated in attempts to help neighbors in need because of this lack of coordination. There was also only limited training available for persons who might want to volunteer but didn't know how. NVOAD emerged naturally in response to these problems in the late 1960s, when leaders of voluntary organizations began talking to one another about greater coordination.[7] W. D. Dibrell of the American Red Cross and other groups such as the Salvation Army led this effort to get voluntary organizations communicating and working together.

In 1970, representatives from seven voluntary organizations came together in Washington, D.C., where they started NVOAD. Those organizations were the American Red Cross, Christian Reformed World Relief Committee, Mennonite Disaster Service, National Catholic Disaster Relief Committee, Society of St. Vincent De Paul, a Seventh-Day Adventist disaster relief group, and representatives from the Southern Baptist Convention. By 1995, the number of member organizations had increased from seven to twenty-six regular members and two affiliates; by 2003, it had reached thirty-five members.[8] NVOAD is an informal organization with most of its functions performed by volunteer efforts contributed by member organizations (until recent years, all NVOAD staff were volunteers). In 1993, in order to facilitate fundraising efforts and allow the development of contracts, a statement of purpose and description of the structure of NVOAD were established and NVOAD became incorporated as a voluntary organization under Virginia law. Soon, various state VOADs began to develop in affiliation with the national organization (by 1994, there were 44 chartered state VOADs), and now virtually all states have them. NVOAD works closely with FEMA and NVOAD's director sits on FEMA's advisory board, allowing NVOAD to express the concerns of the voluntary agencies to leadership at the federal level.

What Does NVOAD Do? NVOAD serves as a point of communication among voluntary organizations engaged in disaster response. It seeks to bring national voluntary organizations active in disaster relief together to foster service that is more effective. NVOAD coordinates planning efforts by these organizations. When a disaster occurs, NVOAD or an affiliated state VOAD attempts to get its members and other voluntary agencies on site to help volunteer organizations work together effectively.

The primary function of NVOAD is communication: "To disseminate information through the newsletter, the directory, research and demonstration, case study, and critique."[8] Communication is also the primary component of the other six priority functions by which NVOAD pursues its mission. NVOAD's primary communication vehicle is its eight-page newsletter, which is distributed three or four times a year and is supported by volunteer labor and funds provided by the Christian Reformed World Relief Committee. In addition to the newsletter, it publishes a NVOAD Organizational Directory that contains the purpose and principles of NVOAD, a statement of structure, conditions for membership, types of membership, and a directory of member organizations. NVOAD has also produced a ten-minute video that describes its role and purposes. Finally, VOADNET is the organization's Internet tool that enables national members and state VOADs to communicate with each other and exchange information.

Besides communication, NVOAD has seven other stated functions: cooperation, coordination (coordinating policy among member organizations; serving as a liaison, advocate, and national voice), education (providing training for member organizations), leadership development (volunteer leader training, especially for state VOADs), mitigation (by supporting federal, state, and local agencies and government legislation), convening function (holding seminars, meetings, board meetings, regional conferences, training programs, local conferences), and outreach (encouraging and guiding regional voluntary organizations active in disaster relief). NVOAD is not itself a service delivery organization and provides no direct disaster relief services.

National Organization for Victim Assistance (NOVA)

NOVA is an organization of victim assistance programs and practitioners, criminal justice agencies and professionals, mental health professionals, researchers, former victims and survivors, and others committed to the recognition and implementation of victim rights and services.[10] Founded in 1975, NOVA claims to be the oldest national group of its kind in the victims' movement. Its mission is to promote rights and services for victims of crime and crisis (including disasters). NOVA serves as a victims' rights advocate in the public policy arena, provides direct services to victims, and helps to train professionals in this area by holding organization, development, and implementation training conferences.

Miscellaneous National and International Organizations

Disaster News Network (DNN)[11] provides the latest and most updated news on disasters in the United States via the Internet. This Web site contains many detailed reports of previous disasters, and its archives can be accessed without fee. DNN is produced by the Village Life Company, an organization founded in 1996 to create content for social justice–related Web sites. DNN receives most of its funding from disaster response organizations.

The Worldwide Disaster Aid and Information Web site (WDAI)[12] provides the latest and most updated news on disasters throughout the world via the Internet. This Web site is a cooperative effort between the American Red Cross, CNN Interactive, and IBM.

The International Critical Incident Stress Foundation (ICISF) is dedicated to the prevention and mitigation of disabling psychological stress following disasters.[13] ICISF provides education and training in critical incident stress management for EMS personnel and for psychologists, psychiatrists, social workers, and licensed professional counselors. ICISF also helps to establish crisis and disaster response programs for different organizations and communities. ICISF is a nonprofit foundation affiliated with the United Nations, American Red Cross, Salvation Army, and incident management stress foundations in Canada, Britain, and Australia.

State and Local Organizations

All states and local communities are required to develop a plan of emergency operations. FEMA has produced State and Local Guide (SLG) 101, which serves as a comprehensive toolbox of best practices, suggested collaborations, and advice on how to prepare for and respond to disasters.[14] This document provides EMS personnel with information on how to develop emergency operations plans (EOP) and includes FEMA's recommendations on how to deal with the entire disaster planning process—from forming a planning team to writing a plan. It also encourages emergency managers to use a single emergency plan rather than relying on separate stand-alone plans. SLG 101 is for state and local emergency management organizations in producing emergency plans to fit any disaster, integrate mitigation into their response and recovery activities, and facilitate coordination with FEMA during disaster situations that necessitate implementation of the Federal Response Plan. *This guide does not include detailed information specific to meeting the mental health needs of disaster victims, which is contained in a separate document* (described later in this section). Addressing spiritual needs is not part of the guide either.

State Emergency Management Agency (SEMA)

SEMAs do at the state level what FEMA does at the federal level but in greater detail and closer to the scene. Although programs in different states vary, I will describe the North Carolina SEMA as an example. This state's SEMA, that is, its emergency management division, is part of the North Carolina Department of Crime Control and Public Safety.

According to the North Carolina SEMA Web site, this division was created by the Emergency Management Act in 1977.[15] Its primary responsibility is to protect the people from natural disasters, human accidents, and terrorist attacks. In 1997, this division was reorganized into six functional units that use the Incident Command System (ICS), the national model for managing emergency operations: Public Information, Hazard Mitigation, Operations, Logistics, Information and Planning, and Finance. The local ICS mirrors the federal ICS structure, helping to streamline and simplify intergovernmental coordination.

Operating out of the administration building in the state capital of Raleigh, North Carolina, and with three local branches located in different areas of the state (Kinston, Butner, and Conover), the North Carolina SEMA responds rapidly to support "first responder" local government emergency operations. The three branch managers and fifteen area coordinators (each of whom is designated on the North Carolina SEMA Web site) are highly trained and have state-of-the-art equipment to respond to the scene of a disaster in order to coordinate SEMA activities. As a result, state resources can be available "within a matter of minutes to assist local governments."

What Does SEMA Do?   The responsibilities of SEMA are largely parallel with those of FEMA but at a more local and hands-on level. The mission statement of the North Carolina SEMA is: "In cooperation with our partners, we are committed to enhancing the quality of life in North Carolina by assisting people to effectively prepare for, respond to, recover from, and mitigate against all hazards and disasters."[16]

Prepare. Public awareness and information programs are conducted throughout the year, including classes on such topics as hazardous materials, search operations, emergency response operations, recovery operations, hazard mitigation, and public information dissemination. SEMA exhibits at shopping centers and conventions and presents programs to interested civic groups. It conducts special workshops on specific threats, such as hurricanes and terrorism, and provides literature, audio-visual materials, and speakers to promote hazard awareness and risk reduction. SEMA also operates the Emergency Alert System with commercial radio and TV broadcasters across the state, who give broadcast time to alert the public when threats become imminent. SEMA and local EMS agencies work as a team to identify and analyze hazards and develop plans of response. These plans address the predictable consequences of disasters: isolated communities, lost power, downed trees, etc., whether from hurricanes, tornadoes, earthquakes, nuclear power incidents, or acts of terrorism. Pre-disaster planning is emphasized so that EMS personnel can focus on evacuation coordination, shelter operations, search and rescue, power restoration, debris removal, and distribution of donated goods. Regular exercises are conducted to improve and streamline responses to disasters and may involve up to full-scale mock accidents involving multiple counties. SEMA also regularly participates with local, state, and federal agencies to test the emergency plans for the state's nuclear power plant.

Respond. North Carolina SEMA's response functions are coordinated from the State Emergency Operations Center in Raleigh. Response functions include (1) setting up area commands located in an impacted region to assist with local response efforts; (2) coordinating central warehousing operations that allow for immediate delivery of bottled water, ready to eat meals, blankets, tarps, and so on; (3) getting into the field deployment teams that assist severely impacted counties; and (4) incident action planning that identifies response priorities and resource requirements twelve to twenty-four hours in advance. The State Emergency Response Team (SERT), which comprises top-level management representatives of each state agency involved in response activities, provides the technical expertise and coordinates the delivery of the emergency resources used to support local emergency operations. When resource needs are beyond the capabilities of state agencies, mutual aid from other unaffected local governments and states are sought through the Statewide Mutual Aid agreement or Emergency Management Assistance compact. Federal assistance may also be requested through the federal Emergency Response Team, which works alongside the SERT in the field during major disasters.

Recovery. In this phase, the focus of SEMA is to restore public infrastructure and damaged facilities and to assist families to obtain safe and secure housing. First, there is an assessment of damages to facilities, infrastructure, homes, businesses, and agriculture. The state recovery team consists of representatives of state, local, and federal emergency response agencies, as well as such organizations as the Mennonites, American Red Cross, Salvation Army, and church groups who coordinate disaster relief and recovery activities. When disaster recovery is beyond the capability of local communities, the governor may use state resources to support recovery operations. When the disaster is beyond the capability of both the local and state resources, the governor may request the president to declare a "major disaster." This authorizes federal financial assistance to supplement state and local recovery efforts. The financial assistance is traditionally a cost share between the federal and state government.

Mitigation. Mitigation involves attempts to minimize the impact that natural disasters have on the population. This usually involves ensuring that homes, businesses, and communities are as safe as possible from damage that could be caused by hurricanes, floods, tornadoes, earthquakes, or other types of natural or technological disasters. Mitigation also involves providing public education about activities that can be done to reduce future loses. Most efforts at disaster mitigation occur at the local government level, which makes laws and regulations concerning growth and development. For example, this might involve requiring certain building restrictions on location and construction of homes in flood-prone areas or emphasizing the importance of flood insurance to people living in at-risk areas. Of the federal funds given to a state that the president declares a disaster area, 15 percent is focused on hazard mitigation. The state administers the program and sets priorities.

State Mental Health Agency (SMHA)

The mental health needs of persons at the state level are the responsibility of SMHAs, and these are the official government agencies in charge of meeting the mental health needs of disaster survivors. The 1974 Robert T. Stafford Disaster Relief and Emergency Assistance Act, which established FEMA, required that all states have a plan to focus on the mental health aspects of disasters. There is a national organization of local SMHA directors (National Association of State Mental Health Program Directors) that advocates for the interests of SMHAs and their directors at the national level. A listing of contact information for SMHAs by state is available.[17]

Until recently, there had been no guidance for SMHAs in responding to the psychological needs of disaster victims. In 2003, The Substance Abuse and Mental Health Services Administration (SAMHSA) of the U.S. Department of Health and Human Services and the National Association of State Mental Health Program Directors collaborated in developing a document to assist SMHAs to plan and implement a response to the mental health needs of disaster survivors and their families.[18] This document, Mental Health All-Hazards Disaster Planning Guidance (also called the Mental Health Disaster Plan Guide or MHDPG), provides direction and advice for state and local mental health leaders to help them create an all-hazards response plan (both the planning process and actual plan content).

The MHDPG includes an analysis of the current status of state disaster mental health plans. Based on a study of thirty-one plans, the authors concluded that most state plans were variable and incomplete. While exemplary plans do exist (Texas and Massachusetts), few states had a single person whose full-time responsibility was disaster and emergency mental health. Many of the states are now revising their plans. As a result, however, the sophistication of SMHA mental health disaster plans varies from state to state.

The MHDPG pointed out a number of limitations of current SMHA disaster plans, including:

- lack of human and financial resources to do the work;
- "back burner" status of disaster mental health planning;
- little political will to focus on disaster mental health planning after a disaster has passed;
- mental health being overlooked in favor of safety and security;
- lack of mental health planning among public safety, disease control, and law enforcement agencies;
- emerging local and regional mental health groups with little knowledge of state disaster mental health infrastructure;
- lack of collaboration and consistency among federal departments and agencies and corresponding state departments and agencies receiving disaster and terrorism funding;
- lack of well-defined, easily implemented mental health disaster programs.

The MHDPG provides recommendations on how to improve state mental health plans, and these are outlined in the document.

What Do SMHAs Do with Respect to Disasters?   The Texas Department of Mental Health and Mental Retardation (TDMR) serves as a model for other SMHAs. TDMR established the State Crisis Consortium (SCC) to coordinate, manage, and ensure the credibility of mental health services to disaster victims and to eliminate duplication of services. The SCC has established a Disaster Assistance and Crisis Response Services Program (DACRSSP) as the lead agency in coordinating mental health responses during disasters.

That response includes providing assessment and evaluation of immediate long-term mental health needs of victims and responders, providing immediate crisis counseling, and coordinating the federal Crisis Counseling and Training programs in federally declared disaster areas. The Texas Department of Public Safety Psychological Services Division provides peer support and victim services to emergency workers and their families, including short-term counseling. The Texas Department of Health Critical Incidence Stress Management Network provides pre- and post-incidence stress management and educational support to emergency response workers. Meeting the mental health needs of disaster victims and responders, then, is coordinated by this central agency (DACRSSP).

Efforts by other organizations or groups (including religious organizations) must be coordinated through this agency. Bear in mind, however, that many states do not have such a centralized system in place to coordinate mental health efforts.

State VOADs

As noted above, nearly every U.S. state now has its own VOAD (Voluntary Organizations Active in Disasters) that coordinates the work of voluntary organizations in that state. These are particularly relevant as an entry point for the work of faith-based organizations. To what extent state VOADs coordinate addressing the mental health needs of disaster victims with state SMHAs is entirely unknown.

Local Police and Fire Departments

Police and firefighters are often the first emergency responders on the scene of a disaster, and can be summoned by anyone by dialing 9-1-1. Their primary responsibility is to ensure the physical safety of the community. Thus, their focus is on rescue and containment of whatever is threatening members of the community. Although all rescue and containment efforts should be performed with compassion and sensitivity, providing formal mental health services or spiritual care is not their responsibility. Such departments, however, may have a chaplain on staff to help meet the emotional and spiritual needs of disaster victims and emergency responders.

Emergency Medical Technicians and Local Hospitals

Local hospitals are the first places that most victims of disasters are transported to. Emergency medical personnel and hospital workers must take care of life-threatening medical needs as their first priority to minimize injury and disability. Mental health issues for both victims and family members often arise after the immediate danger has passed. Thus, hospital nurses, social workers, psychologists, and chaplains are ideally positioned as frontline responders to meet the mental health and spiritual needs of disaster victims brought in for health care.

Summary

An emergency preparation and response system is already in place at the federal, state, and local levels. The focus is primarily on minimizing damage and meeting the *physical needs* of disaster victims. Meeting the emotional and spiritual needs of disaster survivors and EMS personnel, however, is much less well developed. It is essential that contributions from clergy and faith-based organizations fit into the federal, state, and local disaster emergency planning and response to help fill this gap. Before discussing the current activities of FBOs in planning and responding to disasters at the national and the local levels, I will first examine the role that religious faith plays in coping with stress and responding to disasters.

three

Religion and Coping with Stress and Disaster

How often do Americans turn to religion when coping with psychological, social, and situational stress? Is there evidence that religious coping is effective in relieving stress? If effective, how does religion facilitate coping? In this chapter, I first discuss these questions as they relate to stress in general, and then examine studies on religion's role in coping with disaster stress in particular.

Random surveys of the population since 1940 by the Gallup Organization have consistently found religion to be widely prevalent and important to Americans. Surveys over the past five years indicate that about 95 percent of the U.S. population believe in God, more than 90 percent pray, 65–70 percent are church members, at least 40 percent have attended church, synagogue, or temple within the past seven days, and about six out of ten say that religion is "very important" in their lives.[1] Many persons also turn to religion when experiencing stress or feeling fearful or anxious.

Coping with Health Problems

The role of religion in coping with stress has been documented best in persons suffering from health problems. Many studies find that prayer and other personal religious practices are common responses to medical illness and disability. For example, more than seventy studies have now examined the role that religion plays in coping with health problems such as arthritis,[2] diabetes,[3] kidney transplant,[4] hemodialysis,[5] cancer,[6] surviving with cancer,[7] coronary artery disease and bypass surgery,[8,9] heart transplant,[10] lung transplant,[11] HIV/AIDS,[12] surviving with HIV/AIDS,[13] cystic fibrosis,[14] sickle cell disease,[15] amyotrophic lateral sclerosis,[16] chronic pain,[17] and severe illness in adolescents.[18] Regardless of their age, people use religion to cope when they become stressed over their health or the health of a loved one.

The use of religion in this way has frequently been associated with less depression and predicts the development of less depression over time in hospitalized patients.[19] Recovery from depression may also be affected by religion, with religious individuals experiencing more rapid remission of symptoms than those who are less religious.[20,21]

Coping with Loss and Trauma

Other life stresses besides poor health also elicit religious responses. Research indicates that people use religion to help them cope with loss of loved ones, loss of possessions, and loss of security that result from traumatic situations. For example, Maton surveyed eighty-one members of a bereaved parents group (mean age 46, 77% women), dividing them into high- and low-stress samples.[22] Depression, self-esteem, and religious support were assessed using standard questionnaires. High life stress was defined by death of a child within the previous two years (33 subjects) and low life stress if the death occurred more than two years previously (48 subjects). In the overall sample, those reporting greater spiritual support experienced significantly less depression. Effects were stronger in the high-stress group; those with greater spiritual support indicated both less depression and greater self-esteem. In the low-stress group, spiritual support was unrelated to either depression or self-esteem. Thus, religion appears to be particularly important for people during periods of high stress, underscoring its usefulness as a coping behavior.

In another study, this time of older adults, Koenig and colleagues examined the use of religion by one hundred older adults (over 55 years) from North Carolina participating in the Duke Longitudinal II Study of Aging.[23] Subjects were asked how they coped with the worst event or situation in their entire lives, the worst event in the past ten years, and the most difficult aspect of their current lives. Questions were asked in an open-ended format (without mentioning religion in the questions) in order to avoid biasing responses. Forty-nine percent of stressful events were health relat-ed, 29 percent were family related, and 22 percent involved other traumas and losses. Of the 556 different coping strategies, 17 percent were religious in nature, representing the most common category of coping activity. Re-ligious ways of coping were more common among women than men (58% of women used religion to cope with at least one of the three events vs. 32% of men).

There is ample evidence that young people also rely on religion to cope with stress. For example, Mattlin and colleagues examined the cop-ing strategies of 1,556 married people from Detroit, Michigan.[24] Partici-pants were asked what coping resources they used to deal with the most stressful event or situation that occurred in the previous year. A list of coping resources was presented; 55 percent of respondents indicated that religion was used either "some" or "a lot" when dealing with stressors. Religion was used most often when respondents were dealing with more serious stressors having to do with illness or death and less often for mi-nor problems.

Especially important are the results of prospective studies that follow individuals over time to see whether religion makes a difference in their coping. People who suffer the loss of a loved one through death or trau-ma have been studied to determine whether those with spiritual beliefs experience a faster resolution of their grief. In one such study, Walsh and colleagues examined 135 relatives and close friends of patients with ter-minal illness.[25] Standardized measures of grief were administered at one, nine, and fourteen months after the loved one's death. At the fourteen-month follow-up, most subjects who reported no spiritual belief had still not resolved their grief. Those with strong spiritual beliefs, however, re-solved grief symptoms progressively over the fourteen-month period. Strength of spiritual belief remained a highly significant predictor of few-er grief symptoms after other relevant confounders were taken into ac-count.

Religious beliefs may also be used negatively and maladaptively. Some persons feel punished by God, angry at God, or abandoned by God when undergoing negative life experiences that seem senseless and pro-longed. For example, when fifty-eight breast cancer patients talked about the role that religion played in their coping with the illness, the vast majority reported it was helpful and comforting; however, 17 percent used negative emotion words to describe religion's helpfulness.[26] While not common, negative forms of religious coping do occur and are a robust predictor of worse mental health when studied over time.[27] Negative religious coping (as described above) is uncommon among those who are deeply religious and associated instead with infrequent religious practice and low religiousness in general.[28]

As suggested above, the degree to which people use religion to cope varies by the severity of the stressor. Shrimali and Broota compared coping strategies with major and minor surgery between three groups.[29] One group of thirty patients was scheduled for minor surgery, a second group of thirty was scheduled for major surgery, and thirty subjects not undergoing surgery were recruited as controls. Before surgery, belief in God was highest among subjects scheduled for major surgery. After surgery, however, belief in God decreased in the major surgery group but did not change in the other two groups. Thus, as the severity of a stressor increases and sense of personal control diminishes, the likelihood of turning to religion increases. As the old saying goes, "There are no atheists in foxholes."

Ken Pargament from Bowling Green University is perhaps best known for his research on religious coping among persons dealing with non-health-related stress. In his book, *The Psychology of Religion and Coping*, he discusses hundreds of studies that have examined the prevalence of religious coping behaviors and how effective they are in helping people cope.[30] Across a wide range of stressful circumstances, especially during and after severe psychological trauma, turning to religion is a common—almost automatic—response.

Characteristics of Religious Copers

There are certain personal characteristics that help to predict whether or not a person will use religion to cope with stress.[31] Those more likely to do so are older, female, poorer, less educated, ethnic minorities (African American or Hispanic), and immigrants from India, the Arab countries, Hispanic countries, or Africa. Moreover, groups that are more religious may derive greater benefits from religion, as well. For example, Ellison and colleagues surveyed a random U.S. sample of 1,344 African Americans. All subjects were experiencing a major life crisis that caused great mental distress or personal problems.[32] Among the ways of coping that investigators inquired about was the use of prayer, asking the question, "Did you pray or get someone to pray for you?" Nearly 80 percent answered "yes."

Those less likely to turn to religion when coping with stress tend to be younger, male, Caucasian, well educated, healthy, and economically well off. Recent immigrants to the United States from areas of the world such as northern Europe may be less likely to use religion, as well. Consider that weekly religious attendance in Sweden is only about 3 percent,[33,34] and the use of religion to cope with stressful life experiences is reported by only about 1 percent of that population.[35] Similarly, only 50 percent of people in the Netherlands indicate that they are religious,[36] only 43 percent are affiliated with religious organizations, and less than 30 percent indicate that having a strong faith is important.[37] Likewise, in a study of Norwegians who were dying from cancer, 43 percent did not believe in God and 45 percent received no comfort from religious beliefs.[38]

The opposite is true for those in Islamic countries. For example, a study of forty-five cancer patients in Switzerland and forty cancer patients in Egypt found that, whereas only 38 percent of Swiss patients indicated that faith in God and prayer were important sources of support, 92 percent of Egyptian patients reported that God/Allah was significant in helping them to cope.[39]

Thus, religious beliefs and behaviors are commonly used to cope with stresses of all kinds, including health problems, financial stressors, loss of loved ones, and other situational stressors. This is especially true in the United States.

Coping with Disaster-Related Stress

The discussion above addresses the use of religion when coping with stress in general. What about when coping with the stress of natural disasters or acts of terrorism? How does religion facilitate coping with such events? Several early studies indicated that turning to religion, demonstrated by an increase in religious beliefs, was common among disaster victims.[40,41] Even in the 1960s, religious rituals were recognized as a way that many coped with the anxiety and uncertainty surrounding disasters.[42,43] Religious beliefs may be used to explain disasters as a form of supernatural punishment, as was seen after the mid-1960s Trinity River floods in Texas[44] and after Tropical Cyclone Martin hit the Cook Islands in the South Pacific in 1997.[45] In these situations, religion may hinder rather than help recovering victims, although this opinion can be quite controversial.

In a comprehensive review of factors that either mediated or protected against the development of psychopathology following disasters, Gibbs concluded that "contemplative styles of coping—the 'philosophical-theoretical' . . . should also be supported, as this may help the individual find some personal or religious meaning for the disaster."[46] There is evidence people use religion to cope with disaster and often report considerable benefit. This research is reviewed below by type of disaster.

Natural Disasters

1977 Beverly Hills Supper Club Fire

Investigators found that survivors who turned to religion (called philosophical/intellectual coping style) experienced less psychopathology than those who coped by turning to work or drugs (denial) or talking with others about the disaster (interpersonal).[47]

1980s Tornado

North and colleagues examined coping strategies and adjustment of forty-two survivors of a midwestern tornado.[48] Many subjects reported that religious perspectives helped them.

1989 Hurricane Hugo

The most frequently observed coping strategies in this study were talking about the experience (95%), humor (82%), religion (74%), and altruism (47%).[49]

1992 Hurricane Iniki

Investigators found that women were more likely to use religion to cope during and after the hurricane, and religious coping (measured using a 4-item religious coping scale) was positively related to *greater* psychological stress.[50] The positive relationship with religious coping so soon after the disaster, rather than being evidence that religion caused an increase in stress, was probably because stressed individuals were more likely to turn to religion than those who were less stressed. As noted earlier, the greater the perceived distress, the more likely that religion will be used to cope.

1993 Midwest Flood

Smith and colleagues examined religious coping among 209 church members living in the Missouri and Mississippi river basins six weeks following the flood.[51] They also reinterviewed 131 participants six months later to determine psychological outcomes. Many persons reported that religious stories, sermons, the fellowship of church members, and strength from God helped them cope with the difficult life changes brought on by the flood. Smith and colleagues describe members of a small Baptist church who took satisfaction in the fact that while many had lost their homes, they were able to save their church and continue to worship there. Members of the church told the story of a rabbit that found refuge from the floodwaters by escaping behind the sandbags that surrounded the church. The rabbit, whom they named Noah, helped remind them that God would see them through this difficult period.

1997 Hurricane Nigel and Others

Investigators compared responses to hurricane disasters in the Fiji Islands between three different religious groups: Christians, Muslims, and Hindus.[52] Interviews were conducted with twenty members of each group. The findings provide some insight into how religious and cultural differences may influence responses to disaster. Among Fijian Christians, eighteen of nineteen expected their church to help them "get back on their feet," no matter how severe the damage was. In the evident of a hurricane, Christians (often supported by overseas Christian churches) indicated that their church would build new houses for them, supply food and provisions, and provide limited financial aide, regardless of how much government aide was available. Expectations of Hindus and Muslims of their religious communities were less than those of Christians: 75 percent of Hindus and 63 percent of Muslims expected assistance from their temple or mosque. Hindus and Muslims also differed from Christians in what they expected from other members of their religious communities. *Rather than receive anything*, Hindus and Muslims were expected to provide manual labor, food supplies, building provisions, and financial aid to their temples/mosques and to poorer members of their faith community in need of help.

2001 Earthquake

Survivors of a Bhuj earthquake who believed that helping others would lead them to peace and harmony with nature (i.e., improve their karma) experienced greater healing.[53] This effect was especially seen in rural areas.

Acts of War and Terrorism

The United States has been in numerous wars but has not experienced many terrorist attacks on our soil and, as a result, there is less information about how religion helps Americans cope after such attacks. I review what is known below.

1991 Gulf War

Pargament and colleagues followed a group of 215 introductory psychology students at Bowling Green State University two days before the 1991 Kuwait assault (Time 1) and one week after the war stopped (Time 2).[54] These students, who were not involved personally in the war, completed a spiritually based coping scale and measures of mental health at Time 1 and Time 2. Investigators found that while a "pleading to God" subscale was related to negative affect (depressed mood) and to poorer mental health at Time 1, before the assault, it was related to less depression at Time 2, after the assault. Students who coped with stress by "attempting

to lead a more religious life" and those who "expressed discontent with religion" experienced more depression at Time 1, but these coping strategies
were unrelated to mental state at Time 2. Those who coped by "depending
on religious support" experienced less depressed mood at Time 1 and less
global distress at Time 2.

1995 Oklahoma Bombing

Six weeks after the bombing, Pargament and colleagues surveyed 296
members of two churches in Oklahoma City (72% Baptist, 97% white).[55]
Most participants knew at least one person who had been injured or killed
as a result of the bombing; 26 percent actually saw, felt, or heard the blast;
and 12 percent were in a building damaged by the bomb. The question-
naire included twelve items on positive religious coping (i.e., worked together with God as partner to get through; looked to God for strength,
support, and guidance; thought about how one's life is part of a larger spiritual force) and nine items on negative religious coping (i.e., felt the bombing was God's way of punishing them, wondered whether God had abandoned them, questioned whether God really exists, did not rely on God).
Positive religious coping was significantly related to greater stress-related
growth, more positive religious changes (i.e., growing closer to God or the
church), and to *more* PTSD symptoms. Negative religious coping, however,
was more strongly related to PTSD symptoms and to callousness, and was
not as strongly related to stress-related growth or positive religious change,
compared to positive religious coping.

2001 World Trade Center Attack

Most recent on our minds are the events of September 11. As noted
earlier, a cross-sectional survey of the U.S. population in the second week
following the attacks found that 90 percent of Americans coped by "turning to religion" (second only to "talking with others").[56] During the week-
end following the attacks, 60 percent of Americans attended a religious or
memorial service and Bible sales rose 27 percent.[57] Three months following the attacks, 71 percent of the U.S. population indicated that religion
was having an increasing influence on life, a percentage that exceeded all
previous figures since the time when the question was first asked by the

Gallup Organization in 1957.[58] Within three to six months, however, this peaking of American religiosity returned back to its previous level (as anxiety began to subside).

War and Terrorism in Israel

After three years of escalating war and terrorism, a survey was conducted of 314 inhabitants of Tel-Aviv, the West Bank settlement of Kiryat-Arba, and the Gush-Katif settlement in the Gaza Strip.[59] Acute stress and PTSD symptoms were common in the majority of participants, ranging from 61 percent to 85 percent depending on location. In spite of firsthand daily attacks, the residents of the Gaza Strip community (100% of 107 were religious) had the fewest and less severe stress-related symptoms and the highest level of functioning, in contrast to the Tel-Aviv population that was least frequently and least directly affected (where only 24% of 103 residents were religious), which had the most severe symptoms and functional compromise. Religious participants (65%) from the West Bank settlement had the same stress profile as the religious Gaza Strip participants, whereas secular participants had worse stress symptoms than either religious or secular subjects from Tel-Aviv. Overall, religious participants had less acute stress and less PTSD symptoms than secular participants. Among those with acute stress reaction, religious participants had less dissociative symptoms, less intrusive symptoms, and less avoidance. The investigators concluded, "Religiousness combined with common ideological convictions and social cohesion was associated with substantial resilience as compared to a secular metropolitan urban population."

Mechanisms: How Does Religion Help?

There are at least ten reasons why religious beliefs and practices help people cope after disasters, many of which have backing in the research literature.[60] Although expressed largely in Judeo-Christian terms, similar principles exist in other major world religions, although they may be expressed in different language or symbols depending on the particular culture.

1. *Positive worldview.* Religion provides a positive worldview that promotes optimism and coherence. Religion explains things and provides answers. Although those answers may not be satisfying to everyone, for many people they are sufficient. Rather than cold, merciless, and random, the religious world is an orderly place, friendly, with someone in control. That someone is usually a benevolent, kind, merciful, forgiving, and caring Divinity, who responds to prayers and watches over people. Although severe trauma may challenge such beliefs (see below), having them fosters optimism and allows for coherent explanations. Having such explanations, as discussed previously, helps people cope better.

2. *Meaning and purpose.* The religious worldview is one imbued with meaning, and individuals in such a world have a purpose and often a calling. Each human is special and here for a reason. He or she possesses a particular combination of talents and abilities that no one else has. Negative life experiences are viewed as contributing to spiritual growth and maturation. These events, no matter how distressing, can lead to something good or positive. The Christian scriptures say, "And we know that in all things God works for the good of those who love him, who have been called according to his purpose" (Romans 8:28, NIV). There are comparable sayings among the teachings of all great world religions. A major function of religion throughout history has been to enable people to transcend suffering. With meaning, almost anything can be endured. Viktor Frankel, a Viennese psychiatrist imprisoned in a German concentration camp during World War II, emphasized that those who survived the camps were individuals who maintained meaning and purpose in their lives.[61]

3. *Psychological integration.* A religious belief system, by helping to interpret life experiences and giving them meaning and coherence, enables the individual to more readily integrate negative events into his or her existing worldview. Such experiences need to be integrated so that the world can continue to be seen as stable, safe, and predictable. Thus, even when religious beliefs appear to provide harsh explanations that involve punishment and damnation, such beliefs provide a group-sanctioned answer that maintains a coherent world that makes sense. Disaster victims crave for the return of an orderly world and are often not able to move on with their lives until this has been achieved.

4. *Hope and motivation*. Religion provides explanations that foster hope for better times ahead. Again, because good results are always possible for the religious person, this helps combat the hopelessness associated with severe loss and devastation. Even if better times are not possible in this life, there is at least the hope that things will improve in the afterlife. Hope gives people motivation to make the necessary adjustments to adapt to difficult circumstances.

5. *Personal empowerment*. Religion provides personal empowerment by giving those who might otherwise feel helpless and powerless tools to make a difference in their situations. For example, a disaster victim can pray to God for strength to cope with difficult losses, for healing of an injury, for recovery of a sick loved one, for a new job, or for financial resources. Consequently, he or she does not feel as helpless. Instead, the person can now do something (pray) that is believed to make a difference. Knowing that one can talk directly to God, the Creator, the original and ultimate force in the universe, helps to infuse life with power. No longer must a person rely entirely on other people, outside agents, or the random forces of nature to determine his or her fate.

6. *Sense of control*. Religious beliefs give the disaster victim a sense of control that he or she would otherwise not have. Related to the empowerment described above, religion puts control back into the hands of the person. The perceived ability to relate to and influence God helps the religious person regain a degree of control. In that case, it is important to believe that God is indeed in control. Even the belief that God is punishing the person for past sins by allowing traumatic events to occur may still be better than believing that no one is in control. The belief that no one is in control in a situation where one's life or a loved one's life is being threatened can be a source of tremendous anxiety. The religious person feels in control through his or her relationship with God and, in fact, may not need to feel in control because he or she is more able to give up control by "putting it in God's hands." When there is nothing that can be done by the individual to change a situation, then turning things over to God may reduce anxiety and make the person more functional. For this to work, the person must be able to trust that God will take care of things and that God has his or her ultimate best interests at stake. That sense of trust may be al-

tered by severe traumatic events (see below), and pastoral counseling may be needed to reestablish it.

7. *Role models for suffering.* Religious scriptures provide role models for suffering that help people accept their situations and provide solutions for dealing with them. For example, the Book of Job in the Bible describes a man who lost everything—all of his possessions, all of his children, and even his health. This is exactly the situation in which many disaster survivors find themselves. Job responded as most people respond. He became frustrated and angry with God and began questioning God. If a character in the Bible can feel this way, this validates the disaster survivor's feelings. That validation helps to normalize such feelings and makes them less threatening. Furthermore, things turned out well for Job in the end, giving the disaster survivor hope that his or her own situation may also have a happy ending.

8. *Guidance for decision making.* Religion provides guidance for making positive decisions that ultimately reduce stress. For example, severe stress following a disaster may cause a person to drink alcohol or use drugs to numb his or her feelings (which religious beliefs discourage). While alcohol or drugs may reduce stress in the short run, they may lead to addiction and interfere with recovery in the long run. Religious beliefs also encourage decisions to forgive and not hold on to grudges or resentments, helping to maintain social relationships that may be necessary to cope with stress and facilitate recovery. Religion promotes a reaching out to others and encourages people to provide for the needs of others worse off then they are. This, in turn, may help distract disaster victims from their own problems and provide a sense of satisfaction and fulfillment from helping others (as well as increase support from others in their own time of need).

9. *Answers to ultimate questions.* Religion provides answers to ultimate questions that secular culture and science cannot address. Again, "having answers" helps the disaster victim psychologically integrate the negative events he or she may have experienced. As long as the answers lead to positive adaptation and pro-social behavior, it doesn't really matter whether they are the "right" answers (particularly if no right answer can be proven). On the other hand, some religious beliefs may promote aggression or retaliation, in which case religious answers would not be helpful.

Most mainstream, traditional religious belief systems, however, promote forgiveness, acceptance, and pro-social actions.

10. *Social support.* Religion provides social support, particularly for those who are involved in the religious community. Social support is known to reduce the stress of negative life events and to provide practical resources to meet those challenges. Most religions encourage love of neighbor and providing for those in need. Thus, religious beliefs encourage people to care for one another even when it is inconvenient, and promise divine rewards. Furthermore, in religions that believe in a personal God, this becomes another source of support for the individual. The belief in a loving, omnipotent God that protects, cares for, and watches over people, a God with whom one can communicate, provides a powerful partner in dealing with stressful situations.

Summary

Many studies following disasters show that religion is frequently used to cope and often brings comfort and hope that enables survivors to heal and move on with their lives. In this section, I reviewed some of this research and explained how religious beliefs and practices facilitate psychological adaptation to severe trauma. Because of the potential long-term impact of unmet spiritual needs on mental health, expert spiritual care following disaster is important. Mental health counselors should screen victims for spiritual needs and refer them to spiritual caregivers as necessary.

four

The Faith Community's Role during Disaster

The previous chapter examined how individual religious beliefs and practices help to buffer against the effects of stress. What about the faith community, then, as a resource in helping persons affected by disaster? To what extent are clergy and faith-motivated volunteers actively involved in helping survivors during and after these events? In this chapter, I review what is known about the role of clergy in providing mental health care in general and more specifically during disasters. The role of volunteers from the faith community will also be addressed, although much less information is known about this group.

It is clear from an examination of the literature, perusal of Internet Web sites that contain disaster-related articles, and speaking with disaster experts, that religious organizations have formally or informally responded to disasters for a very, very long time. Many of those activities, however, go unnoticed and unacknowledged by the formal disaster response system. For example, Quakers and Mennonites have responded to disasters throughout the United States for over fifty years, and many of the mainline religious denominations and their social service agency extensions have had formal disaster preparation and response programs in place for the past fifteen to thirty years. At the local level, faith-based organizations have been involved for hundreds of years, perhaps dating back to the plague epidemics in Europe during the sixth century A.D.,[1] when early Christians often cared for the sick.[2]

Role of the Clergy

There is evidence that ministers and congregations can play a significant role in responding to the social and psychological needs of survivors of disasters.[3,4] Given that four out of ten people seek counsel from a member of the clergy when having a personal problem (according to a University of Michigan national survey),[5] it should not be surprising that clergy are often the first ones contacted by trauma survivors. Interestingly, in that University of Michigan study, individuals who experienced a crisis involving the death of somewhat close to them were almost five times more likely to seek aid from the clergy than from mental health professionals.

A number of other studies document the role that clergy play in counseling Americans facing stressful life situations. For example, data from the NIMH Epidemiologic Catchment Area study, the first large-scale survey of psychiatric disorders in the United States, indicated that the emotional disorders people sought help for from clergy were of the same severity (major depression and anxiety) as those disorders typically seen by mental health professionals.[6]

Psychologist Andrew J. Weaver has calculated the amount of mental health services that the clergy deliver each year compared to the amount of services provided by members of the American Psychological Association. According to the U.S. Department of Labor, there are approximately 350,000 clergy serving congregations in the United States, including 4,000 rabbis, 49,000 Catholic priests, and 300,000 Protestant ministers.[7] Clergy report that they spend about 15 percent of their 50-hour workweek counseling members of their congregations.[8] This means clergy spending nearly 140 million hours delivering mental health services each year. That figure amounts to the 83,000 members of the American Psychological Association delivering services at a rate of 33.2 hours per week. Not included in this figure, Weaver notes, is the counseling done by nearly 100,000 full-time Catholic sisters, thousands of brothers in religious orders, or clergy from Buddhist, Hindu, Muslim, and other religions.

Clergy from minority populations are particularly active in providing counseling and other mental health services to their members. A survey of clergy from New Haven, Connecticut, revealed that the vast majority indicated they did crisis counseling, especially African American clergy. Researchers concluded, "Parish-based clergy, especially the black clergy, function as a major mental health resource to communities with limited access to professional mental health services."[9] Other studies report that African American ministers are often involved in the counseling of individuals at high risk for PTSD, such as the homeless, persons abused as children, victims of domestic violence, alcohol or drug abusers, and those with diseases such as AIDS.[10] Mexican Americans are also quite likely to seek mental health assistance from members of the clergy. In a study of 534 persons in El Paso, Texas, investigators found that they were most likely to seek help for personal problems from clergy (41%) than from any other professional; after clergy, they sought help most frequently from medical doctors (29%), psychiatrists and psychologists (21%), and social service agencies (18%).[11]

Besides addressing the emotional needs of disaster victims, clergy and pastoral counselors are the only professionals competent to address the spiritual needs that arise after unexpected catastrophes that strike down the young and the old, the healthy and the sick, the affluent and the poor—devastating entire communities.

Religious Presence during Disasters

A number of studies document the important role that clergy and faith communities play in responding to natural disasters and terrorist attacks.

Natural Disasters

1970 southwestern tornado. Nelson and Dynes surveyed 663 persons in a southwestern town eight months after it was hit by a tornado that caused massive damage.[12] Data on several religious characteristics were obtained in order to determine their impact on helping behaviors following the tornado. Frequency and importance of prayer, frequency of religious attendance, and self-perceived religiosity were all positively and significantly correlated with providing emergency funds to relief organizations, goods to tornado victims, and disaster relief services to those needing help. Frequency of attendance at religious services, in particular, was related to emergency helping, and this effect was independent of age, income, and congregational friendships. Investigators concluded that religious bodies are particularly helpful when they provide concrete opportunities for members to reach out to disaster victims (i.e., giving information on how, when, and whom to help).

1974 Kentucky tornadoes. Between April 3 and April 4, 148 tornadoes struck eleven states during a sixteen-hour timeframe. Twenty-six of these hit the state of Kentucky, resulting in seventy-seven deaths, 1,337 injuries, and over $110 million in property damage. Approximately five years after this disaster, Chinnici investigated the role of clergy during the aftermath.[13] Eighteen clergy were chosen from a town in Kentucky where 2 percent of the population was killed, 10 percent hospitalized, and 95 percent were directly affected in one way or another by death/loss resulting from the tornadoes. Many of the clergy whose own families and homes were affected by tornadoes experienced problems themselves, grieving over lost possessions, experiencing fear of future storms, dealing with guilt over surviving, coping with jealousy toward others who were not affected, experiencing anger at God, and even going through divorce. The tasks of the clergy were many, including holding and attending funeral services, holding religious services, visiting people in the hospital, spending time with people who were affected, providing counseling and support for victims, raising money and distributing it to victims, handing out food, helping at temporary morgues, helping in the medical clinic, opening their church to those without homes, serving as director for the local Red Cross chapter, and becoming directly involved with rebuilding churches, homes, and other disaster relief services. Overall, however, the ministers interviewed in this study did not appear very tuned into the emotional and spiritual needs of disaster survivors. Chinnici also observed, "The relationship between pastoral problems [of victims] and an attempt on the part of the pastor to provide counseling services was extremely poor." Only six of eighteen ministers were involved in counseling.

1985 West Virginia flood. Although Chinnici did not find that ministers were very helpful following the Kentucky tornadoes, others have reported just the opposite. On November 4 and 5, 1985, a major flood hit several sections of West Virginia and Virginia, killing fifty-four people, causing 4,300 families to evacuate, and resulting in nearly $1 billion worth of damage. Between seven and sixteen months after the floods, Echterling and colleagues surveyed twelve ministers from a rural area in West Virginia and twelve ministers from urban Roanoke, Virginia (population 96,000), areas that were heavily affected.[14] The findings are particularly detailed and provide a unique window on the role that the clergy play in responding to disasters. Ministers from the two areas were matched on denomination, age, sex, and extent of loss suffered from the floods. They were involved in many aspects of both immediate and long-term relief, including rescuing people at risk; helping clean up; providing food, clothing, and shelter; organizing programs; generating and distributing donations; and, especially, offering emotional support. Ministers first focused on the needs of their own congregations and then broadened their efforts into the general community.

Differences were noted between the roles of rural and urban ministers: urban ministers tended to specialize in a particular area (i.e., coordinating an interfaith committee, working with families of flood victims, catching victims who fell through the cracks of the regular emergency response system), whereas rural ministers were more likely to remain generalists, serving a variety of roles (since their communities were often without any formal emergency response services). Rural ministers often turned their churches and homes into disaster shelters and centers for distribution of water, food, clothing, and meeting other basic needs.

Urban ministers were more attuned to "the system" already in place, and were more likely to make referrals to mental health services, social services, or other agencies. They were also more likely to become involved in advocacy, either through legal or political systems, to ensure that survivors' needs were met. Urban ministers perceived one of their greatest challenges as "working with different denominations with different flags to wave." They also spent a lot of energy checking the legitimacy of requests for assistance, since most individuals requesting assistance were strangers (less of a problem among rural ministers, who often knew personally those seeking help). Both urban and rural ministers, however, had difficulties allocating funds and deciding who should have the greatest priority (with rural ministers having to decide between friends and neighbors).

Rural ministers were commonly looked on as community leaders, since they were often the only professionals who were readily present and respected by most of the people. Rural ministers continued their involvement in relief long after the disaster had ended, often canceling vacations to help those in need. At the time of the survey, seven to sixteen months after the floods, many of the rural ministers were still quite involved in relief work.

Meeting the emotional needs of flood survivors was another common task of both urban and rural ministers. They listened to the stories of families in their congregations and made an informal assessment of need for emotional support, comforting those who needed help in grieving over losses. Even more important and unique was their role in meeting the spiritual needs of survivors who struggled to integrate the tragic events into their theological belief systems.

Members of the congregation weren't the only ones who suffered traumatic stress after the floods. Many of the ministers themselves, especially from rural areas, experienced symptoms of post-traumatic stress: two-thirds experienced fatigue, 58 percent felt burned out, 58 percent felt guilty about not doing enough, 42 percent felt more irritable, 42 percent experienced problems with concentration, one-third reported intrusive memories, and one-quarter felt numb and easily startled. These symptoms were less than half as common among urban ministers. As noted earlier, rural ministers played many more roles in responding to the disaster and were more personally involved with survivors than were urban ministers, who placed higher priority on their activity as "directors" or "coordinators" (thus maintaining more emotional distance from the situation).

Researchers concluded that ministers play a major role in a community's response to disaster by serving to mobilize and organize key resources. This involves not only providing basic necessities and meeting physical needs but, more importantly, performing rituals, giving sermons, and offering individual counseling that enabled survivors to find meaning in the face of suffering. However, ministers themselves need support and rest following a disaster, including professional counseling in many cases. Knowledge of the unique and overlapping roles that rural and urban ministers play in responding to disasters can help disaster counselors better meet the psychological needs of clergy.

1993 Midwest flood. Between May and September of 1993, record flooding occurred across North Dakota, South Dakota, Nebraska, Kansas, Minnesota, Iowa, Missouri, Wisconsin, and Illinois, resulting in fifty deaths, 72,000 homes damaged, 36,000 square miles affected, and over $10 billion worth of damage to crops and property. During this time, churches in small towns served as places where affected families could sleep and receive food and clothing. It was in churches that volunteers often gathered to organize and carry out relief activities to help flood victims.[15]

1997 Tropical Cyclone Martin. Mental health counselors and clergy have not always worked smoothly together following disasters. The Cook Island community of 23,000 islanders was deeply religious (made up primarily of Christian Church, Mormon, Catholic, and Seventh-Day Adventist congregations), with religious teachings underpinning much of the administrative and social functions of the island. In the aftermath of Cyclone Martin, conflict arose between trauma therapists and local clergy.[16] Therapists disagreed with the clergy's explanation that the cyclone was caused by the people's departure from paths of righteousness and punishment from an angry God. Even politicians became involved, attributing the disaster to the community's failure to attend church regularly, to working on Sundays, and to paying too much attention to the island's pearl industry. Therapists argued that this approach was not helpful to those grieving over their dead and attempting to cope with losses, and pointed out that this response might further impair the sense self-esteem of survivors.[17] However, it is not known whether the damage caused by guilt over supernatural explanations outweighed the positive effects of having a clear explanation for the event and distinct rituals for dealing with its cause, since no measures of mental health were administered.

2005 Hurricane Katrina. Clergy throughout the country were involved in organizing the delivery of immediate practical assistance to victims and in helping survivors piece their lives back together in the months following the disaster. Within less than a week after the hurricane struck, news reports began appearing about the activities of churches in disaster relief.[18] The Web sites of virtually every religious group ranging from Muslims to Buddhists to fundamentalist Christians were soliciting donations and asking for volunteers to help in this effort. It will be years before we have objective information on the scope of these activities; however, it is safe to say that the amount of immediate and long-term assistance will rival in volume that provided either by the U.S. government or by secular private relief organizations (i.e., United Way).

War and Acts of Terrorism

Stress of war in 1990s. Chaplains are frequently called on to help soldiers cope with the psychological stress associated with war. Zimmerman and Weber examined a program to help chaplains themselves deal better with the stress of caregiving in such situations, and also to improve their effectiveness in the field.[19] Thirty-one chaplains involved in NATO and United Nations military missions carried out in the 1990s were involved in a series of workshops that covered such topics as PTSD, vicarious trauma, coping techniques, spirituality, self-care, and family issues. The program was so successful that it has become a normal part of troop deployments in various parts of the world.

1995 Oklahoma City bombing. Brad Yarbrough, clergy coordinator for the Oklahoma City Family Assistance Center, spoke at a June 17, 2002, conference (sponsored by the American Red Cross and New York City Disaster Interfaith Response) prompted by the September 11 terrorist attacks.[20] He provided information on what his organization learned from the Oklahoma City bombings. The coordination of spiritual care at the time of the bombings was made easier by an extraordinary coincidence. Apparently, the mayor's downtown prayer breakfast with local religious leaders concluded just before the bomb blast and many ministers were still available on the spot. As a result, the ministry effort was organized immediately, with an organizational structure that had the authority of the mayor's office. Thus, from the beginning, ministers were supervising ministers. That supervision involved screening clergy and religious volunteers to ensure that they were integrated into the overall response. Ministers were instructed "to graciously adhere to the tenets of their faith with the top priority of providing compassionate care to the affected." The worry of EMS personnel was that ministers would be too "preachy" at a time when individuals were vulnerable and needed compassion. This worry, according to Yarbrough, did not materialize, and even mental health professionals were impressed by the clergy's response.

A report by EMS personnel who directed the disaster response to the Oklahoma City bombing explicitly recommended seven years after the event: "Clergy are an important component to the process. Include clergy in your plan to deal with family members not only to identify victims, but also [to] stay with the families while they are trying to locate loved ones."[21]

2001 World Trade Center attack. Clergy were direct responders to September 11, both during and after the events. They prayed with rescue workers, performed last rites over bodies, searched for victims, held prayer vigils, and supported victims' relatives in family assistance centers throughout the affected parts of the city. A national poll conducted a few weeks following the attack showed that Americans were more likely to seek help from a spiritual caregiver than from a physician or mental health professional.[22]

The Ground Zero Clergy Task Force (GZCTF), organized by the Northeast Clergy Group (NEC), grew to include 250 ministers from the region and crossed denominational lines.[23] GZCTF helped in the creation of the Clergy Crisis Responders program at the NYC Mayor's Office of Emergency Management. This program gave clergy access to Ground Zero, family assistance centers, and respite areas throughout the boroughs. It provided bilingual critical incident and post-traumatic stress training, offered debriefing sessions for clergy responders, and directed them to respite resources including retreat centers, counseling, and support groups. In partnership with Northwest Medical Teams and others, NEC also gave financial assistance to underserved victims, subsidies to victims needing qualified professional counseling, and resources for case management services to families. Finally, the group initiated an Internet-based clearinghouse of Christian resources to provide clergy and lay people with information on how to match their resources to victims' needs.

In addition, local city churches hosted at least a thousand short-term volunteers from around the country in the year following September 11, directing them to tasks at Ground Zero and throughout the city.

Challenges

The primary role of the faith community is the provision of pastoral care. Pastoral care includes addressing significant psychological as well as spiritual issues. A major challenge involves how to work in partnership with other disaster relief agencies rather than in competition with them, and how to avoid duplicating services (provided by other relief agencies and faith-based organizations). The key here is "partnership"—how to develop working relationships with local partners before a disaster occurs. FBOs provide a key role in mobilizing response efforts. Remember, there are over 350,000 local congregations that include nearly 70 percent of the U.S. population. Thus, the faith community has tremendous potential in responding to disasters at the local level. What is most essential, however, is that it is not done in a haphazard, uncoordinated manner. When the latter occurs, there is considerable likelihood that the faith community's response will be seen more as a burden and a liability than as a resource.

During the emergency phase of a disaster, victims receive a great deal of attention and support. Soon, however, funding and attention begin to diminish as basic needs are addressed and safety is restored. The process of disaster victims putting their lives back together, however, has only begun. Little support is provided by emergency response services during long-term recovery. The Red Cross, for example, makes quite explicit that they do not provide support in the long term but rather only emergency mass care services. During the recovery phase, however, faith communities have the opportunity to walk alongside disaster victims as they go through the very difficult process of adaptation and moving on. It is then that pastoral care often becomes so important. This represents a key component of "continuation" of care, where disaster response personnel begin to "hand off" responsibilities to local faith communities.

Pastors need to know about the kinds of resources available to them in the community, particularly as this relates to skills that they do not have. In the same way, disaster response personnel need to understand the special skills and abilities that religious leaders have and the resources that local congregations can provide.

Summary

Clergy play a distinct and critical role in disaster response. Those roles differ in urban vs. rural settings. Although clergy and mental health professionals have worked peaceably side by side following many disasters, there is the potential for conflict, which has been observed in some situations. Just like EMS personnel, clergy who are actively involved in disaster response work need support and sometimes counseling themselves. Much less in known about what role hands-on volunteers from the faith community play in disaster response, since very little research has included them. Nevertheless, many religious organizations have disaster response programs that provide an opportunity for members of congregations to become actively involved in disaster relief. Organization of this response and communication between all sectors is critical to avoid duplication of services and conflict.

five

Faith-Based Organizations Involved in Disaster Response

FBOs play a major role in disaster response, often serving right alongside local, state, and federal EMS workers. This chapter focuses on the disaster response arms of national faith-based groups that help organize local faith-based responses. Although this book is on how FBOs meet the emotional, social, and spiritual needs of disaster victims, these efforts are usually not separated from general disaster relief and recovery services. Most of these organizations are motivated by compassion and the desire to relieve suffering. As a result, mental and spiritual needs are met hand in hand with physical needs and basic necessities.

Selected Larger Faith-Based Disaster Response Groups

Adventist Community Services (ACS)

ACS operates under a "memorandum of understanding" with FEMA, the American Red Cross, and many local SEMAs in providing a range of services to disaster survivors, their families, and communities.[1] These services include emergency distribution of relief supplies (drinking water, groceries, blankets, etc.) through relief centers located in high school gyms or churches, warehouse operations for donated goods (from groups, corporations, and individuals who want to provide goods or volunteers), community collections (working with radio stations, churches, and civic groups to gather donated goods), and disaster child care (providing training and supervision of volunteers to work in temporary day care centers for young victims of disasters as their parents reorganize their personal affairs). ACS also provides listening posts and door-to-door visitation that address the emotional and spiritual needs of disaster victims, their relatives and neighbors, doing so through interfaith groups of pastors and trained lay pastoral workers.

American Baptist Men (ABMen) Disaster Relief

The mission arm of the American Baptists is the ABMen disaster relief team, which participates in relief efforts such as floods and tornadoes.[2] When a disaster strikes, "point men" act as scouts and try to visit the community that has been hit by the natural disaster to see if it is feasible to send ABMen disaster relief volunteers. The organization belongs to National Voluntary Organizations Active in Disasters (NVOAD) and coordinates its work with other volunteer relief efforts.

American Red Cross, Disaster Spiritual Care Services

The American Red Cross, while not a faith-based organization, does have its own spiritual care division. In fact, the Red Cross is the designated organization responsible for providing for the spiritual needs of disaster victims according to the Aviation Disaster Family Assistance Act of 1996. This act created a team of professional chaplains who were given responsibility for organizing and administering protocols by which community clergy could provide spiritual services to disaster victims. Guidelines for providing spiritual care at disaster sites were developed, including training programs, a code of ethical conduct, and a certification process. The Red Cross has spiritual care chaplains who provide nondenominational prayers and blessings over the dead found at disaster scenes. These chaplains play a major role in many Red Cross disaster response operations.

When airplane disasters occur, members of the Red Cross's Spiritual Care Aviation Incident Response Team work with spiritual leaders in the local community and specific religious organizations, including the Association of Professional Chaplains, the National Association of Catholic Chaplains, and the Association for Clinical Pastoral Education.[3] After the September 11 terrorist attacks, the Red Cross spiritual care team was an integral part of the ongoing recovery operation—supporting families who had waited months for their loved ones' remains and EMS workers who had witnessed many gruesome scenes.[4] The team recruited and coordinated the activities of over nine hundred community clergy (25% from outside the New York City tri-state region) who volunteered to provide emotional and spiritual support to survivors, families, and rescue workers.[5] Nine months after the attacks, the American Red Cross brought together rabbis, imams, monks, priests, and nearly one thousand other New York–area religious leaders at a conference entitled "The Lifecycle of a Disaster: Ritual and Practice" to address the task of helping members of affected congregations rebuild their lives.[6]

Ananda Marga Universal Relief Team (AMURT)

Ananda Marga ("path of bliss") is a Hindu religious organization, with its primary U.S. office in Rockville, Maryland. AMURT describes itself as one of the few non-government relief and voluntary organizations of Third World origin.[7] AMURT's objectives are to aid the poor and underprivileged through disaster relief, redevelopment programs, and community service, including meeting the needs of disaster victims in the United States. AMURT has maintained a long-established working relationship with the Red Cross as well as with other disaster relief and other development organizations in the United States and abroad.

Catholic Charities (CC) Office of Disaster Response

Catholic Charities USA is an arm of the Catholic church, which is the largest religious denomination in the United States. As one of the nation's largest faith-based social service agencies, CC provides social services to people in need regardless of religious, social, or economic background. The Office of Disaster Response, in operation since 1990, gives grants of $10,000 for immediate emergency relief to local CC agencies to provide shelter, food, clothing, counseling, or other emergency services to those who have lost homes or been temporarily displaced. These funds can be used for both emergency and long-term assistance to disaster victims. For example, CC recently gave $30,000 to help victims in the October 2003 fire in southern California that took sixteen lives, destroyed 2,000 homes, and forced tens of thousands of people to evacuate. Likewise, CC took up donations from around the country to help victims of Hurricane Isabel, which smashed into the North Carolina and Virginia coasts in September 2003. The CC disaster response Web site also provides brochures for schools, businesses, families, and parishes on how to plan and respond to disasters.[8] I could not locate information on whether CC addresses the mental health or spiritual needs of disaster victims, although this is likely included in their general response through local CC agencies.

Christian Disaster Response (CDR)

The mission of CDR, which is a branch of the American Evangelical Christian Church (AECC), is disaster relief in the United States and internationally.[9] By pre-training, training, and organizing local church members, CDR prepares AECC churches to respond to domestic disasters. The group cooperates with the American Red Cross, the Salvation Army, NVOAD, and Church World Service to place their members in volunteer assignments during disasters. CDR responds on a denominational level with an On-Site Disaster Assessment Program conducted by trained CDR volunteers, but it is made available only if requested by qualified agencies. CDR provides direct assistance to victims using mobile and fixed-site kitchen/feeding facilities and "in-kind" disaster relief supplies from member churches across the United States (which stockpile food, clothing, building materials, medical supplies, etc.). I could find no information on the CDR Web site that specifically addresses spiritual or mental health issues.

Christian Reformed World Relief Committee (CRWRC)

CRWRC is a relief, development, and educational ministry supported by the Christian Reformed Church in North America. With its national office split between Ontario, Canada, and Grand Rapids, Michigan, CRWRC supports a hundred staff and many programs that respond to the needs of underprivileged individuals "in Christ's name."[10] One of its five aims is "Relief and Disaster Response through working in ways that maintain and/or build long-term community development during the relief, rehabilitation, and reconstruction phases."

Church of the Brethren Disaster Response (CBDR)

CBDR provides volunteers to clean up debris and to repair or rebuild homes for disaster victims who lack sufficient resources to hire a contractor or other paid labor.[11] Formerly called the Brethren Disaster Services, the CBDR program was originally part of the Brethren Service Commission established in 1941. CBDR volunteers are often present at disaster sites. During the devastating floods brought on by Hurricane Agnes in 1972 that inundated Maryland, Pennsylvania, and Virginia, Brethren Disaster Services responded with 2,203 volunteers who assisted 725 of the affected households in Wilkes-Barre, Pennsylvania.

Church of Jesus Christ of Latter-Day Saints

The Humanitarian Service division of the church sends food, clothing, medical supplies, and other emergency relief assistance following disasters.[12] The relief efforts of LDS are coordinated through their Humanitarian Center in Salt Lake City, where it provides employment and job training for 130–140 workers at any given time, many of them refugees from other countries.

Disciples of Christ Week of Compassion (WOC)

WOC provides emergency and long-term assistance to disaster victims following hurricanes, floods, earthquakes, droughts, civil war, and other natural and human catastrophes. This group responds to a disaster about once every two days.[13] To accomplish its goals, WOC partners with the Church World Service, Action by Churches Together, Interchurch Medical Assistance, Food Resource Bank, Heifer Project International, Volunteers in Mission, Refugee and Immigration Ministries, and hundreds of local DOC churches in the United States and around the world. WOC lists disaster-related activities on its Web site detailing the organization's involvement in specific disasters.[14]

Episcopal Relief and Development (ERD)

Over the past sixty years, ERD has provided "emergency assistance in times of disaster, rebuilds devastated communities after the immediate crisis is over, and offers long-term solutions to help people sustain healthier, safer, a more productive lives."[15] Its mission is to bring together the generosity of Episcopalians and others with the needs of the world by raising funds for disaster relief. As an immediate response to a disaster, ERD provides technical expertise and funding for food, water, shelter, and other basic necessities to Episcopal churches in affected areas. In terms of rehabilitation, ERD works with local communities to construct new buildings, replant crops, restore clean water systems, and repair clinics and schools damaged by the disaster. In terms of finding long-term solutions, ERD is also involved in the support of schools, job training programs, and health care facilities in partnership with local Episcopal churches. Again, as for most other groups described above and below, there is little mention on the ERD Web site about addressing emotional or spiritual needs.

Friends Disaster Service

Friends Disaster Service, Inc. is an outreach ministry of the Religious Society of Friends (Quaker). Organized in 1974, the Friends Disaster Service consists of volunteers who help provide relief following disasters.[16] The Friends Disaster Service is funded solely by an annual auction and by donations from supporters. All money received goes directly toward relief efforts in disaster-stricken areas. The group provides the needed labor, tools, and expertise, as well as counseling and support in times of crisis (one of the few religious groups that actually specifies this). Friends Disaster Service works with other national disaster relief organizations in responding to disasters and helping recovery efforts. FDS has organized units of volunteers in several, but not all, states.

International Aid

International Aid describes itself as a distinctly Christian, Bible-based relief and development agency that provides global relief, development, and training. It engages local churches in programs of compassion, that is, in tangible projects of mercy that restore the physical, emotional, and spiritual health of needy persons.[17] "Local church" means the Body of Christ as expressed as an organized institution of the Christian church worldwide. International Aid assists families and communities in coping with emergencies and helps them regain a sense of self-sufficiency. When responding to Hurricane Floyd, International Aid volunteers helped to restore over six hundred homes in affected areas. Similarly, when tornadoes hit western Michigan, International Aid mobilized forty volunteers who assisted families in the cleanup efforts. The organization belongs to the Association of Evangelical Relief and Development Organizations (AERDO) (see below).

Lutheran Disaster Response

LDR is one of the largest national religious groups that specifically emphasize counseling and mental health services for disaster victims, including spiritual care. LDR is a cooperative ministry of the Evangelical Lutheran Church in America (ELCA) and the Lutheran Church–Missouri Synod (LCMS). According to its Web site, LDR seeks to minister to the urgent needs of people who are affected by a domestic natural disaster or terrorist activity.[18] LDR receives its financial support from ELCA Domestic Disaster Response and LCMS World Relief. LDR's mission is to "demonstrate Christ's compassion for people by promoting health, healing and wholeness for disaster survivors." LDR attempts to help survivors of disasters through a coordinated, community-based system involving all Lutheran entities, both local and national.

Mennonite Disaster Service (MDS)

The mission statement of MDS is to serve as a "channel through which various constituencies of the Anabaptist churches can respond to those affected by disasters in North America. While the main focus is on clean up, repair and rebuilding homes, this activity becomes a means of touching lives and helping people regain faith and wholeness."[19] Mennonites have been known for barn raising and conducting harvest bees as ways of putting their faith into practice when fellow church members or neighbors face disaster. After responding to tornadoes in Oklahoma and flooding in Manitoba in 1950, Mennonites began to further organize their practice of providing disaster relief. However, it was not until 1993 that MDS was formally incorporated. That same year, Mennonite volunteers were involved in the response to Hurricane Andrew and the Midwest floods. MDS has grown rapidly in its disaster-response capabilities; it now involves more than three thousand Mennonite, Amish, and Brethren in Christ churches and districts. MDS has opportunities for both short-term and long-term volunteers in responding to disasters, and seeks donations to support these volunteers.

Nazarene Disaster Response (NDR)

NDR is a national network of disaster volunteers supported by the Church of the Nazarene. It provides volunteers, assisted by trained district, regional, and national leaders, who cooperate with other national, state, and local EMS teams to meet the needs of disaster victims.[20] Under NDR's direction, local Nazarene churches responded to the fires in Southern California, to Hurricane Isabel, and to the recent tornadoes in the Midwest and Southeast, distributing hundreds of "crisis kits" to meet basic needs of survivors. Nazarenes were also active relief workers after the 2001 World Trade Center attacks. NDR has articles on its Web site discussing how to help disaster victims suffering from stress and grief, what to say to children when explaining disasters, and how to develop a family disaster plan.

Northwest Medical Teams International (NWMTI)

NWMTI is a Christian organization that is committed to demonstrating "the love of Christ" to persons of need, upholding Christian values in their work.[21] The group is nondenominational and welcomes volunteers of different faiths. Volunteers contribute by working in the NWMTI warehouse, at home, and in satellite offices. Volunteers may participate on short-term mission teams and by assisting the work of the organization in the field. NWMTI had its origins when businessman Ron Post saw a picture of a dying Cambodian refugee on television and felt the need to make a difference. Soon, Post led a group of twenty-eight medical volunteers to care for the survivors of Cambodia's killing fields, and out of this effort developed NWMIT. Teams of volunteers have traveled throughout the world and to areas of the United States when needed, including to New York City on September 11.

Presbyterian Disaster Assistance (PDA)

PDA, a branch of the Presbyterian Church USA, seeks to provide a ministry of "relief and response to national and international disasters, aid to refugees and displaced persons, refugee resettlement, and efforts toward development" ("Structural Design for Mission," General Assembly minutes, 1988, p. 15).[22] This ministry is carried out through partnerships with other religious denominations, related church agencies, middle governing bodies, and local congregations. PDA's focus is on assisting the local church in times of disaster, recognizing that people and organizations will come and go during and following disasters but the local church will stay in the community to continue to love, support, give help, and heal wounds. For example, during the 2003 Southern California fires, PDA leaders worked with the Church World Service, FEMA, and the American Red Cross in linking churches and presbyteries to address the needs of the most vulnerable populations within the fire zone.

Reformed Church World Service (RCWS)

RCWS is a missions program of the Reformed Church in America. In response to World War II, it joined with several other denominations in 1946 to form the Church World Service (CWS) (see below). RCWS's primary mission is to fulfill the biblical mandate of Matthew 25 to feed the hungry, welcome the stranger, clothe the naked, care for the sick, and visit the imprisoned.[23] RCWS accomplishes this in part by providing emergency relief to disaster victims and others in need of immediate assistance, by participating in recovery efforts to help people who have lost their homes and jobs, and by encouraging development of long-term solutions. RCWS works with the CWS and Action by Churches Together, responding to their appeals for emergency relief by deployment of disaster consultants and volunteers. It also participates in rehabilitation of disaster victims, including providing food pantries and soup kitchens, and volunteers to help get them back on their feet. RCWS also seeks to influence public policy through advocacy.

Salvation Army (SA)

The SA has local, regional, and national disaster services programs with disaster response teams who are ready to be dispatched to disaster locations. These teams are coordinated and directed by SA officers and trained personnel and are supported by "on call" volunteers. They may be the first at the scene to "serve those in need, at the time of need, and at the place of need." SA provides mass mobile feeding; collects, organizes, and distributes donated goods; and provides temporary shelter and medical assistance.[24] For example, it was the SA that responded to the nation's first major disaster in 1900, when a hurricane devastated Galveston, Texas, leaving more than five thousand people dead and virtually destroying the city. The SA sent members from across the country and raised funds to provide both material and spiritual assistance.[25] The SA has been a key partner with the American Red Cross in responding to many disasters, and helped to form NVOAD in its early days.

Southern Baptist Disaster Relief (SBDR)

SBDR is one branch of the Southern Baptist Convention North American Mission Board (which exists "to proclaim the gospel of Jesus Christ, start New Testament congregations, minister to persons in the name of Christ, and assist churches in the United States and Canada in effectively performing these functions"). SBDR has more than twenty thousand people who are trained to provide relief, and serves more than a million meals each year to disaster victims.[26] For example, SBDR was recently involved in the 2003 West Virginia flood (including Ohio and Kentucky). Its feeding units provided over 7,000 meals and 67 showers to flood victims, and a "mud-out" team helped to dig people's homes out of mudslides. In the California wildfires, SBDR provided 84,677 meals and 3,110 showers. As part of providing meals, the organization provides emotional and spiritual support to disaster victims.

United Church of Christ National Disaster Ministries (UCCNDM)

UCCNDM is a program of the Wider Church Ministries board and is coordinated through the church's Office for Global Sharing of Resources.[27] It cooperates closely with the Church World Service (CWS), participates in the CWS executive committee, funds CWS's Emergency Response Office, and trains volunteers as local disaster resource consultants. The UCCNDM works locally through its thirty-nine regional conferences, each drawing on the gifts of its local congregations and serving as ecumenical partners when disasters occur in their area. This involves pre-disaster planning as well as post-disaster cleanup and reconstruction. They coordinate their relief efforts closely with community EMS groups.

Unitarian Universalist Trauma Response Ministry (UUTRM)

The UUTRM is composed of Unitarian Universalist ministers, lay members of the church, and others who support the vision and beliefs of Unitarian Universalism.[28] Trained in disaster response, they provide direct on-site ministry at disaster sites, crisis counseling for disaster victims, hospitality and respite care, debriefing and other stress management services, and administrative infrastructure for disaster response. They also provide multi-faith spiritual care to survivors of disasters and education of congregations on culturally sensitive spiritual care for disaster victims. UUTRM is supported by a grant from The All Souls Church of New York City Emergency Relief Fund. All Souls Church is one of the nation's largest Unitarian Universalist congregations.

United Methodist Committee on Relief (UMCOR)

UMCOR is a humanitarian agency of the United Methodist Church operating in more than a hundred countries that provides aide to refugees and provides relief in disaster areas.[29] In 1972, UMCOR became an institutionalized unit of the church and part of the General Board of Global Ministries. It has responded to earthquakes in Nicaragua, hurricanes in Haiti, famine in Africa, and domestic tornadoes and floods in the United States. While focusing on disaster relief and refugee resettlements, UMCOR's emphasis has also been on eradicating the roots of hunger and poverty, with several programs establishing training schools to give individuals the skills to become educationally and economically self-reliant. UMCOR regularly offers both pre-disaster and post-disaster training to the denomination's regional conferences. A number of regional conferences of the UMC are actively involved in disaster response coordination (including the Dakota Conference[30] in Fargo, N.D.; Louisiana Conference in Fayetteville, La.; and Whitesburg Conference in Whitesburg, Ky.).

United Jewish Communities (UJC)

UJC represents 156 Jewish federations and 400 independent Jewish communities across North America.[31] UJC is one of the world's largest networks of faith-based social service providers and programs, dedicated to safeguarding and enhancing Jewish life. A secondary emphasis is to meet the needs of all people, Jews and non-Jews, wherever they live (including during times of disaster). UJC came about when the Council of Jewish Federations, the United Israel Appeal, and the United Jewish Appeal all merged. UJC promotes meaningful giving of finances, hands-on voluntarism, and a shared commitment. The focus is primarily on the Jewish federation community. UJA-Federation of New York played a major role in disaster relief following September 11.

Volunteers of America (VOA)

VOA describes itself as a "spiritually based organization providing local human service programs, and opportunities for individual and community involvement."[32] The group's motivation for helping people originates from its Christian heritage; the organization was founded on Christian values. However, it sees itself as a meeting ground for people of all faiths united in service. VOA serves more than a million people each year, including abused children, at-risk youth, the frail elderly, people with disabilities, the homeless, and other needy persons. VOA is also a major provider of skilled long-term nursing care and health services. The organization's emergency services division seeks to help those experiencing emergency situations, and I would assume this includes disaster survivors (although this is not explicitly stated on the VOA Web site). VOA addresses immediate needs of people and offers long-term support when necessary.

World Vision

World Vision is a Christian humanitarian organization in operation since 1950 whose purpose is to "transform the lives of the world's poorest children and families."[33] The group responds to sudden natural disasters and slow-building humanitarian emergencies around the world, seeking to provide relief by pre-positioning emergency supplies for immediate response and remaining after the crisis to rebuild and restore communities.

Coordinating Faith-Based Efforts

This is only a partial list of FBOs that provide disaster relief, and many, many more such groups exist. However, most of the major ones have been included above. Next, I describe FBOs that, rather than provide direct services, organize the efforts of FBOs that do.

There is obviously a great deal of interest among faith-based organizations in helping disaster victims and emergency workers. This large potential source of resources and volunteers, which is desperately needed during disasters, should be utilized as fully as possible without duplicating services, obstructing or complicating the work of emergency personnel, mismatching resources with needs, or allowing such resources to go unused because of frustration and barriers to "getting into the system." Thus, there is great need for mobilization and coordination of these faith-based efforts. Several organizations already exist that are attempting to improve communication and coordination of services provided by faith communities and other volunteer organizations responding to disasters. In alphabetical order, these include Action by Churches Together (ACT), the Association of Evangelical Relief and Development Organizations (AERDO), Church World Service Emergency Response Program (CWS), and National Voluntary Organizations Active in Disaster (NVOAD).

Action by Churches Together (ACT) International

According to its Web site, ACT "is a global *alliance* of churches and their related aid agencies working to save lives and support communities during emergencies. . . . ACT works through 195 Protestant and Orthodox churches and related aid agencies from the membership of the World

Council of Churches (WCC) and the Lutheran World Federation (LWF)."[34] The ACT Coordinating Office is funded entirely through member contributions. In 2002, ACT raised $43.8 million for humanitarian assistance to people recovering from disasters in forty-eight countries. ACT seeks to help victims of natural and environmental disasters and emergencies caused by war and civil conflict. ACT provides assistance to all persons irrespective of religious belief, nationality, or ethnic origin. ACT and its members sign the "Code of Conduct in Disaster Relief" of the Red Cross and abide by SPHERE standards (Humanitarian Charter and Minimum Standards in Disaster Response).

Association of Evangelical Relief and Development Organizations (AERDO)

AERDO describes itself as "a professional forum for non-profit Christian agencies and individuals engaged in relief and development work. AERDO exists to promote excellence in professional practice; to foster networking, collaboration and information exchange; and to enable its membership to effectively support the Church in serving the poor and needy."[35] Founded in 1978, AERDO represents a network of forty-five evangelical Christian relief and development agencies in North America. The board of directors is made up of representatives from each member agency. Its member agencies primarily include evangelical groups that seek to feed the hungry and carry out other humanitarian efforts that include meeting the needs of disaster victims. However, it is not clear that this is its primary purpose, as with NVOAD and CWS. Nevertheless, there is almost no overlap between member organizations of this group and those with NVOAD or CWS.

Church World Service Emergency Response Program (CWS)

CWS,[36] part of the National Council of Churches of Christ in the U.S.A., is an ecumenical relief and development agency whose members include thirty-five Protestant, Anglican, and Orthodox national denominations. CWS's goal is to bring about a cooperative faith-based community response to disaster in the United States. It seeks to: "Participate as a witness to the Gospel of Jesus Christ in timely and effectively meeting the physical, psychological, and spiritual needs of communities affected by natural and human-caused disasters—particularly those that are marginalized."[37] CWS is one of the two most recognized coordinators of major faith-based disaster activities to date. Member organizations include:

African Methodist Episcopal Church
African Methodist Episcopal Zion Church
Alliance of Baptists
American Baptist Churches USA
The Antiochian Orthodox Christian Archdiocese of North America
Armenian Church of America (including Diocese of California)
Christian Church (Disciples of Christ)
Christian Methodist Episcopal Church
Church of the Brethren
The Coptic Orthodox Church in North America
The Episcopal Church
Evangelical Lutheran Church in America
Friends United Meeting
Greek Orthodox Archdiocese of America
Hungarian Reformed Church in America
International Council of Community Churches
Korean Presbyterian Church in America
Malankara Orthodox Syrian Church
Mar Thoma Church
Moravian Church in America
National Baptist Convention of America
National Baptist Convention, U.S.A., Inc.
National Missionary Baptist Convention of America
Orthodox Church in America
Patriarchal Parishes of the Russian Orthodox Church in
    the U.S.A.
Philadelphia Yearly Meeting of the Religious Society of Friends
Polish National Catholic Church of America
Presbyterian Church (USA)
Progressive National Baptist Convention, Inc.
Reformed Church in America

Serbian Orthodox Church in the U.S.A. and Canada

The Swedenborgian Church

Syrian Orthodox Church of Antioch

Ukrainian Orthodox Church in America

United Church of Christ

The United Methodist Church

CWS helps the faith community play a significant role in disaster mitigation, preparedness, and response by identifying the unmet needs of survivors (particularly the vulnerable and marginalized), providing emotional and spiritual care (in addition to physical rebuilding), assisting in long-term recovery, restoring and building community relationships, and serving in an advocate role. CWS assists communities responding to disasters, helps to resettle refugees, advocates for fair national and international policies, educates volunteers, and offers volunteer opportunities. CWS consultants help to organize interfaith coalitions in affected areas following disasters. The CWS Emergency Response Program enables its member organizations to effectively work together and work with CWS partners (Red Cross, etc.). When disaster strikes, CWS encourages all religious organizations to coordinate efforts with others in the faith community to provide efficient, effective assistance for those in need.

National Voluntary Organizations Active in Disasters (NVOAD)

NVOAD serves as a point of communication among voluntary organizations engaged in disaster response. It seeks to bring national voluntary organizations together to foster more effective service to people affected by disaster in terms of cooperation, coordination, communication, education, mitigation, and outreach. NVOAD coordinates planning efforts by many voluntary organizations responding to disaster. When a disaster occurs, NVOAD or an affiliated state VOAD attempts to get its members and other voluntary agencies on site to help volunteer organizations work together effectively. The primary function of NVOAD is communication: "To disseminate information through [its] newsletter, [its] directory, research and demonstration, case study, and critique."[38] Besides communication, NVOAD has seven other stated functions: cooperation, coordination (coordinating policy among member organizations, serving as a liaison, advocate, and national voice), education (providing training for member organizations), leadership development (volunteer leader training, especially for state VOADs), mitigation (by supporting federal, state, and local agencies and government legislation), convening (holding seminars, meetings, board meetings, regional conferences, training programs, local conferences), and outreach (encouraging and guiding regional voluntary organizations in disaster relief). NVOAD is not itself a service delivery organization and provides no direct disaster relief services. Although not a religious organization per se, twenty-three of its thirty-five member organizations are faith-based groups, even after excluding the American Red Cross as a faith-based group. Member organizations that are faith-based include:

> Adventist Community Services
> American Baptist Men
> Ananda Marga Universal Relief Team
> Catholic Charities USA
> Christian Disaster Response
> Christian Reformed World Relief Committee
> Church of the Brethren General Board
> Church World Service National Disaster Response
> The Episcopal Church
> Friends Disaster Service
> International Aid
> Lutheran Disaster Response
> Mennonite Disaster Services
> Nazarene Disaster Response
> Northwest Medical Teams International
> Presbyterian Church (USA)
> The Salvation Army
> Society of St. Vincent de Paul
> Southern Baptist Convention
> United Jewish Communities
> United Methodist Committee on Relief
> Volunteers of America
> World Vision

NVOAD and CWS are probably the most recognized coordinators of major faith-based disaster activities at this time.

State Coordinating Groups

Faith-based state disaster response organizations. There are also a number of faith-based groups at the individual state level that seek to co-ordinate disaster responses, including the Florida Interfaith Networking in Disasters[39] (Orlando), Missouri Interfaith Disaster Response Organization[40] (Ashland), Metro Jackson Interfaith (Clinton, Mississippi), Bdecan Presbyterian Church and Tribal Home Improvement and Health (Warwick, North Dakota), Appalachian Habitat for Humanity[41] (Robbins, Tennessee), Disaster Recovery for the Diocese of Galveston-Houston[42] (Texas), and North Carolina Interfaith Disaster Response.[43]

Faith-based activities through state VOADs. A number of local VOADs have been developing their spiritual capacities.[44] For example, the president of the Ohio VOAD recently organized the training of chaplains with basic disaster counseling skills for work within the incident command structure. This has helped to prepare chaplains to respond to disasters and identify those who are qualified in disaster situations. Similar efforts to involve faith-based organizations are being initiated by staff at the Colorado and Montana VOADs.

State mental health associations (SMHA). SMHAs have been given the charge of meeting the mental health needs of disaster victims. To what extent all SMHAs are prepared to do this on both a short-term and long-term basis, however, is not clear. Furthermore, there is substantial potential for conflict if SMHAs see efforts by FBOs to meet the psychological and spiritual needs of disaster victims as untrained people trying to invade their turf. However, this does not have to be the case. For example, during the Durango (Colorado) fires, many of those needing evacuation were members of mental health groups, leaving few resources available to address the psychological needs of disaster victims.[45] Lutheran Disaster Response got involved by obtaining a SAMHSA contract to provide licensed counselors to meet those needs. Individuals requiring further intervention were then referred to local mental health specialists for psychological treatment or to local clergy for more spiritual help. In this way, LDR worked together with the Colorado state mental health association in meeting the psychological and spiritual needs of disaster victims.

Summary

Almost every major religious group in the United States has a disaster response arm that goes into action when a disaster strikes. The largest of these are Lutheran Disaster Response, Catholic Charities, and the Salvation Army. The American Red Cross also has a spiritual care team of chaplains who respond to airplane disasters and other incidents, but only in the short term. Finally, there are several FBO coordinating groups on both national and state levels that seek to improve communication and collaboration between faith communities responding to disaster.

six

Coordinating Faith-Based Efforts at the Local Level

Although there is much that national FBOs do in response to disasters, what exactly happens in terms of organization and coordination of faith-based efforts at the local level during and following disasters is not always consistent. As noted earlier, lack of coordination runs the risk of duplication of services or even conflict with other agencies responsible for disaster response. Many factors bear on what actually occurs at the local level, including the type and scope of the disaster, the particular congregation (including the emphasis placed in their theology on helping), relationships between congregations in the area, how much the congregation has been affected directly, the size of the community, and the ready availability of formal emergency relief services.

In small-scale disasters that don't get the attention of the broader community through widespread media coverage, there is often a heavier reliance on local resources. If emergency services are not well developed or they become overwhelmed, then the involvement of clergy and religious congregations may soon occur. Participation by individual religious congregations, particularly those not directly affected by the disaster, will vary depending on the extent to which they see responding to other's physical, social, and psychological needs as part of their mission. For those congregations who see evangelism as their primary mission (vs. caring for the sick and needy), this will be emphasized more or less during relief efforts and may affect involvement in long-term recovery activities, as well. Since congregations in a particular area will likely have a wide variety of religious beliefs and motivations, there is also the issue of competition and conflict over who will lead and coordinate relief efforts.

Because an over-arching factor affecting faith community involvement will depend on the size of the community, the coordination of local faith-based efforts below for communities of four different sizes—small
(under 10,000), moderate (10,000–50,000), large (50,000–500,000), and major
metropolitan centers (greater than 500,000)—is discussed below. Descrip-
tions of the unique situation in each type of community and examples of
disaster response are provided.

Small Town and Rural Areas (under 10,000)

In small communities, there may be a small police department,
county sheriff, and/or county fire department. These departments are unlikely to have a chaplain or pastoral counselor on staff to address the needs
of trauma victims. There may be anywhere from one to twelve churches in
the area (considering that there are at least 353,000 religious congregations
in the United States with one congregation for every 827 persons).[1] The
nearest hospital is likely located in a nearby town of larger size. In such
communities, where resources are limited, the clergy and faith community
are often at the heart of disaster response, both in the short term and in
the long term. People living in small rural communities tend to know one
another personally and in general are more religious than those living in
urban areas (75% of those in rural areas are church members compared to
66% in urban areas).[2] Many rural communities are built around a church
or churches.

For example, rural ministers in the 1985 West Virginia floods were
often the community leaders in disaster relief efforts. They provided shelter in their churches for homeless victims and distributed food and basic
necessities. A similar phenomenon occurred in the 1997 Ohio River flood.
The rural river town of New Richmond, about twenty-five miles east of
Cincinnati, was dramatically affected.[3] The population of the town (2,800)
fell about 25 percent after the flood. The faith community provided housing for elderly and disabled people but there were not many resources
available for other disaster survivors, according to Dean Griffith, pastor of
the Mount Zion–St. Paul United Church of Christ. Griffith, a representa-

tive of the Ohio Conference United Church of Christ Disaster Recovery team, helped lead the New Richmond Community Improvement Corporation, which assisted in the town's recovery efforts.

The experience of the New Richmond community initiated a discussion among clergy and EMS responders concerning the role of the faith community. In small communities, FBOs can assist in many ways. One may be helping disaster victims navigate through government paperwork and regulations to get disaster relief funds. According to Christian Disaster Response (American Evangelical Christian Church) Executive Director Ron Patterson, "They [disaster victims] really need someone to walk them through that so they don't have to fight the government." Patterson also suggests that the faith-based community help educate people about the dangers and problems of living and building in flood plains, which would go a long way in mitigating future flood damage. Reverend Griffith agrees that the faith-based community is in a good position to fulfill this educational role because people rely on clergy when disaster strikes. He strongly recommends that church leaders be included when dialogues about flood disaster mitigation by EMS leaders take place. Barbara Yagerman, a FEMA public affairs officer, agrees: "Churches can come to the table as partners in the community to define roles and responsibility. The federal government alone can't make the nation safe from disaster, and neither can states or local governments."[4] In small communities, then, involving religious leaders in disaster planning, response, and mitigation is essential.

Small to Moderate-Size Town (10,000–50,000)

A moderate-size town will have fairly well-developed police and fire departments, and perhaps a member of the local clergy will serve as an "on-call" chaplain. It is likely to have only one hospital, since there is an average of one hospital per 50,000 people in the United States.[5] That hospital will probably have a full-time trained chaplain on staff. Such a community is likely to have twelve to sixty religious congregations.

Even in moderate-size towns, clergy and faith communities continue to play a major role in helping disaster victims and their families cope during a disaster recovery period. Following the March 2001 school shootings in Santee, California (population 52,000), which left two students dead and eleven wounded, the faith community continues to help residents struggle with the "why" question as they seek to find meaning in this disaster. Such events also give rise to religious questions of a broader nature. According to Rev. Jerusha Neal from a local United Methodist church, "People saw that shooting as so much bigger. . . . This problem was not isolated around one kid who did the wrong thing as much as it is a broader question of what's going on with the young people in our community . . . what was causing this young boy so much pain and how do we make this a safe place for the rest of the community."[6]

Individual clergy from religious congregations that are directly affected by a disaster continue to play a major role in easing spiritual and psychological recovery of affected members. However, victims may come from many different denominations (or churches within the same denomination), and there can be competition between clergy (who may not know each other) on which religious group should lead relief efforts. Given this possibility, a particular member of the clergy is ideally positioned in small to moderate communities to coordinate the faith communities' efforts, the local hospital chaplain. Because established connections already exist between the community hospital and the other local disaster response systems (including the police, fire department, and Red Cross), the hospital chaplain could easily fill the coordinator role—especially if there is only one hospital in the community. The hospital chaplain already has contacts both with the local disaster response system and with many of the churches in the area; furthermore, he or she is seen as a relatively "neutral" clergyperson in the community. Thus, the chaplain might be the best person to coordinate disaster preparation and response among local religious bodies. If there is more than one hospital or one chaplain, a decision will need to be made on who will take the lead.

For example, Ed Dininger (Ed.Dininger@fhmd.org), chaplain of Florida Hospital in Ormond Beach (population 35,000), obtained training in disaster planning and response by attending a course on critical incident stress management. He then brought together a disaster response team based at the Ormond Beach hospital consisting of a psychologist, nurse, and several area clergy. There is also a second hospital in the area, a county hospital. Chaplain Dininger knows the chaplain in that hospital well, and even though their hospitals are somewhat competitive for patients, there is good cooperation at the pastoral care level. Dininger has been having meetings between his team, the local Red Cross, and fire and police departments as part of disaster preparation. Since he has contacts with many local community clergy who help provide chaplain services at the hospital, Dininger is well known and trusted; therefore, he has been accepted as the disaster response coordinator.

Moderate to Large Town (50,000–500,000)

Police and fire departments are usually well staffed in these communities, and the larger ones may actually have a part-time or full-time trained chaplain on staff. In such communities, there will be from one to ten hospitals, each with its own chaplain staff, and from sixty to six hundred religious congregations, making competition between groups a major barrier that needs to be overcome to achieve cooperation and coordination of relief efforts. Leadership by any one clergyperson is unlikely to be successful; teams of clergy will be required to coordinate efforts.

Recall that during the 1985 West Virginia floods urban ministers in Roanoke, Virginia (population 96,000), tended to specialize in a particular area, were more likely than rural ministers to make referrals to mental health services, social services, or other agencies, and often served an advocacy role to ensure that survivors' needs were met. Urban ministers typically didn't know disaster victims personally, nor did they know individually the many EMS workers involved in the disaster relief effort. As expected, urban ministers perceived working with other ministers from different denominations as one of their greatest challenges. One minister remarked, "It was very difficult working with different denominations with different flags to wave."[7] Thus, cooperation and coordination of faith-based disaster relief efforts become a major priority in middle-size communities.

Large City or Metropolitan Area (greater than 500,000)

In large urban areas of this size, there will be at least ten hospitals, each with one or more full-time, highly trained chaplains. City police and fire departments are top of the line in quality; typically, they have a full-time chaplains on staff.

In the 1995 bombing of the federal building in Oklahoma City (population of 506,000), Jack Poe, chaplain of the Oklahoma City Police Department, was actively involved from the start in counseling people traumatized by the bombing. Poe arrived on the scene fifteen minutes after the blast and worked for the next twenty-one days straight.[8] Not only the victims needed Poe's help. He started out providing pastoral care to victims at the scene but soon was helping police from his department, health care workers, funeral directors, morgue volunteers, and members of the National Guard. He also counseled victims when a tornado that struck Oklahoma City in 1999 left many victims homeless or injured.

Community clergy were also involved in helping survivors after the Oklahoma City bombing. This included specially trained teams from Presbyterian Disaster Assistance who offered spiritual and emotional care to victims and their families. However, because there may be from five hundred to five thousand religious organizations in such communities, it is essential to carefully coordinate FBO disaster relief efforts. Disaster relief arms of large national religious bodies (such as Presbyterian Disaster Assistance, Lutheran Disaster Relief, Catholic Social Services, and others) are helpful in such situations because they direct local activities by their member congregations. It is also important to involve an overall volunteer coordinating body such as NVOAD, ACT, or CWS.

There may also be reasons to form a task force of clergy working on the scene, as occurred following the September 11 World Trade Center attacks. Recall that clergy formed the Ground Zero Clergy Task Force (GZCTF), which grew to include 250 ministers from many different denominations in the region.[9] GZCTF helped in the creation of the Clergy Crisis Responders program at the NYC Mayor's Office, which helped coordinate FBO efforts throughout the city during the disaster aftermath.

In Washington, D.C., following the attacks on the Pentagon, the Church World Service (CWS) likewise worked with local clergy and officials to form an interreligious recovery task force.[10] The task force included the chaplain from the Pentagon, the head chaplain of the U.S. Coast Guard, and many local clergy. Shirley Norman, who headed the CWS effort, observed that victims who don't know about available help often turn to faith leaders, as do those who might be afraid to seek help elsewhere in coping with disaster-related feelings of stress. Another goal of the interreligious task force was to counteract any racism towards people of Middle Eastern descent. For large communities such as this, forming a task force of influential religious leaders from the affected community to brainstorm about how to go about educating local clergy on how to respond is an essential first step to increase the effectiveness of faith-based relief efforts.

Importance of Individual Congregations

Although FBO disaster relief efforts and clergy task forces are important in large cities, there may be individual boroughs that function in many ways like small towns—each with one or two clergy who may be recognized as community leader(s) (and who may not recognize the authority of other FBO disaster relief groups). This is especially true in minority communities, where the religious leader has much more power than in European Caucasian neighborhoods. Emergency management personnel and faith-based disaster relief groups must recognize such community religious leaders and make efforts to enlist their cooperation; otherwise, relief efforts may be significantly hindered.

Summary

The level of involvement and the coordination of faith-based efforts at the local level depend largely on the size of the community. In small communities of less than 10,000, the clergy will likely play a major role in disaster relief, including the meeting of psychological and spiritual needs, and should therefore be directly included in EMS planning and response. As the size of communities grow and number of religious organizations increases, the need for coordination of the faith-based response increases. In small to moderate-size communities (10,000–50,000), the local hospital chaplain may be the best person to serve this coordinating role. As communities become still larger (greater than 500,000), there may be many hospitals and hundreds or thousands of religious congregations, requiring coordination by larger FBO-coordinating bodies and, in some instances, by the formation of local clergy teams. Given that the Red Cross may see the meeting of spiritual needs as its primary responsibility and that local mental health authorities may see the meeting of psychological needs as their responsibility, coordinating local faith-based efforts with these agencies becomes essential. Even in large urban centers, however, leaders of individual congregations may play a major role in the community's receptiveness to EMS, Red Cross, mental health, and sometimes even FBO-coordinating group personnel. Thus, such local religious leaders should be contacted and their cooperation sought.

seven

Preparing Faith Communities for Disaster

What do faith communities need to know in order to prepare themselves for a disaster that might strike their area? Such information could be necessary not only for their own survival, but also for their ability to meet the psychological, social, and spiritual needs of disaster victims in their congregations or broader community. What kinds of support or pastoral care interventions are likely to be most effective? Practically, how might faith communities go about developing a disaster plan for their own congregations? These are questions that I will try to address here.

Information Needed

There are eight areas that FBOs need information about in order to effectively respond to disasters:

1. how to develop a disaster plan;
2. how to partner with other disaster response organizations;
3. education about disaster risks in their area;
4. understanding their role during disasters;
5. understanding their assets and the assets of other disaster response groups;
6. flexibility during times of disaster;
7. setting up town meetings after disasters; and
8. preparation to serve as spiritual guides and counselors.

First, FBOs need to know what is included in a disaster plan and how to go about developing one. When disaster strikes, faith communities should be prepared so that they will not be the needy ones. In this way, faith communities can provide a witness of care and concern to the community at large rather than drain resources needed by others. I have included an example of a disaster plan at the end of this section (and a more detailed one in the Resources section on pages 129–34 about addressing mental health needs).

Second, according to FBO experts in disaster response, congregations need to know how to collaborate effectively with national and local disaster relief agencies (especially since funding may be available from them). On the national level, this includes being connected with their denominational disaster response arms. For example, Lutheran congregations should be connected to Lutheran Disaster Response, Southern Baptist congregations to Southern Baptist Disaster Relief, and Jewish congregations to United Jewish Communities. Each of the national denominational groups have a Web site where information can be obtained, including specific information on disaster planning and response activities. The Federal Emergency Management System (FEMA) may in the future have representatives from faith groups on its board (or may already have them). On the local level, this means seeking to partner with local "players," including agencies such as the State Emergency Management Agency (SEMA), Red Cross chapter, State Mental Health Association (SMHA), state Voluntary Organizations Active in Disasters (VOAD), and, of course, local police and fire departments. Such partnerships need to be developed before disaster strikes so that faith committees, volunteer groups, and secular EMS groups can get to know one another and establish working relationships beforehand.

Third, faith communities should seek education. What are the disaster risks in their area—is it hurricanes, tornadoes, fire, terrorist attacks, nuclear reactor leaks, etc.? Faith communities should seek information about the kinds of psychological reactions that disaster victims experience. When are psychological, social, and spiritual needs are greatest? When are victims most receptive to the kinds of resources that faith communities can offer? Who are those at greatest risk for Post-Traumatic Stress Disorder

(PTSD)? What are the early symptoms and signs of PTSD, depression, or other short-term and long-term emotional problems? Faith communities need to know what kinds of problems can be handled in the local faith community, how best to handle them, which problems need to be referred to specialist mental health providers and when to do so. Knowing who those mental health specialists are (especially by getting to know them beforehand) is essential.

Fourth, each faith community should define its role and let others know about it. There are many misconceptions among mental health professionals and other secular EMS agencies on what role the faith community can play following disasters. In particular, faith communities can offer non-proselytizing pastoral care services to help address issues of meaning and purpose and address other spiritual needs of victims that EMS workers and counselors are not able to address. Faith communities may already have programs in place helping certain subgroups of the population (running a shelter for the homeless, for example). When disaster strikes, because these helping relationships existed beforehand, FBOs may be especially effective in meeting the psychological, social, and spiritual needs of particular groups. Other EMS agencies need to know about these special relationships and the competencies that faith communities can provide.

Fifth, faith communities need to "map" their own assets and the assets of other agencies and community organizations involved in disasters. For example, does a faith community have a food pantry, a day care center, a large building that could be used as a temporary shelter, etc.? Is there already a Stephen's Ministry or other trained volunteer group within the faith community that provides psychological and social support to others—the sick, the poor, the distressed? These groups may be natural sources of support for people following disasters. Of course, in order to avoid duplication of services and possible competition and conflict, faith communities need to know what services other faith-based and secular agencies are providing (and how large their capacity for providing such services are). Furthermore, when disaster strikes, the faith community itself may benefit from the services of secular EMS groups, so prior knowledge and connections with these groups will be helpful.

Sixth, faith communities need to be flexible during times of disaster. The disaster may disable certain community EMS agencies, requiring that the faith community take up the slack if it is able. For example, mental health services may be in such great demand following a disaster that mental health organizations are overwhelmed. Faith communities may need to take up this slack by providing at least temporary support to those in need and directing persons with more severe emotional problems to specialist providers.

Seventh, the faith community could be responsible for setting up townhall meetings following a disaster to identify resources and coordinate response efforts. This is especially true for small towns or rural areas where access to emergency medical services may be limited. In those communities (small towns or boroughs of large cities), clergy are often the best known and most respected of those who are in natural leadership positions.

Eighth, when disaster strikes, pastors and faith community leaders should be prepared to serve as spiritual caregivers and guides to disaster victims both within and outside their congregations. Clergy are uniquely qualified to address questions related to the meaning and purpose of life, what this means for them spiritually, and how to find new hope in order to rebuild their lives. Certain pastoral care approaches may be more effective than others, and the timing of the approaches may be crucial.

Faith-based Support Following Trauma and Disaster

Based on his years of experience as a member of both the clergy and the mental health profession working with disaster victims, Francis Gunn provides specific recommendations on how to serve as a spiritual caregiver. Here, "spiritual caregivers" are defined as members of the clergy, pastoral counselors, or any trained volunteers who assist others with pastoral/spiritual support.[1]

There are many roles, which spiritual caregivers can assume to support those impacted by disaster or traumatic events. These include direct care such as crisis counseling, a compassionate and supportive presence, facilitating prayer and hospitality, and care on behalf of those in need through advocacy and serving as a link for information and referral services. The following guidelines are helpful:

1. Safety and Security

Recognizing the importance of safety and security, the spiritual caregiver needs to reassure survivors that they are out of harm's way: "You are safe now, you are safe here, nothing is going to happen to you." Assuming a relaxed, reassuring posture, making eye contact, and touch can be helpful when you sense it is appropriate.

2. Active Listening

Listening is especially important because survivors need to "ventilate," to tell what happened and how they are feeling. Active listening is a process whereby statements are validated in such a way that it encourages the speaker to continue sharing and communicates that you are hearing and validating what they are saying.

3. Use of Silence

Sometimes periods of silence will take place as survivors explore their feelings and thoughts from within. Gentle, open-ended questions and validating responses can be helpful as well as allowing for natural breaks of silence.

4. Non-judgmental Approach

It is important to be non-judgmental even if people say things that might strike you as inappropriate or shock you. You may correct inaccurate information (if you have the correct information) but be careful about speculating and making statements that you do not know to be true that survivors may hold you to later.

5. Ventilation

Let people tell you how they feel and avoid telling them "I know how you feel" since it is very likely you do not. Avoid telling people that everything is going to be all right unless you know that to be true. In most cases it is too premature to predict such a thing and it tends to move people away from sharing how they truly feel.

6. Assess Spiritual/Pastoral Resources

Assess what spiritual/religious resources are already available to people. Good pastoral care helps people access the spiritual resources they already have before attempting to directly provide or "be the resource."

    a. Is there a faith community that they have a relationship with?

    b. Are there clergy they might want to be contacted?

    c. In difficult times, do they find it helpful to pray? Would they want you to offer a prayer with them?

    d. Attempt to assess what immediate needs they may have for companionship and/or spiritual support.

7. Use of Scripture and Prayer

Some people may feel comforted by Scripture passages being read. Others may want to offer specific prayers. Some will be comforted simply by the assurance that you will pray for them. Let them take the lead in suggesting what they find to be comforting and helpful. Prayer should never be imposed and should take as generic a form as possible when you are not entirely clear about a person's faith tradition and its manner of praying.

8. Ministry of Presence

Often the best thing we can do for survivors is to "be with them" in a supportive and compassionate way. Ask them what they need. Spiritual caregivers may not be able to provide certain "hands on" help but we can be with people as they clean up from damage, notify relatives, make funeral arrangements, etc. We may tend to their needs for hospitality and immediate concerns such as offering them something to drink or a blanket or coat, etc.

9. Advocacy

When necessary, spiritual caregivers may also recommend to survivors that they seek additional help such as medical, mental health support, childcare assistance, etc. Unless a situation is life threatening this is best done by offering several options if available. Spiritual caregivers can also serve as liaisons between survivors and available services, especially when people are hesitant to accept those services.

10. Empowerment and Choices

Sometimes well-meaning relatives, friends, or neighbors may try to take charge and begin telling survivors what they need to do. Let survivors know that they can make choices around accepting the advice of others. Encourage them to inform others about what is helpful to them and what is not helpful. You may gently advocate on their behalf when necessary. Often those who want to help do not know what to say or do to be helpful and will be receptive to your guidance.

11. Volunteer Assistance

Provide volunteer assistance when helpful. Sometimes faith communities have volunteers who can help with preparing and delivering meals, doing errands, and companionship. Always check out whether such assistance would be welcome. Avoid offering help that you cannot provide.

12. Death Notifications

Assist with death notifications both in the initial notification and continuing notification process with other relatives, friends, neighbors, and faith community members.

13. Assistance with Funeral Preparations

Often clergy and pastoral ministers are the first people who are turned to for assistance in scheduling and planning funerals.

14. Ongoing Bereavement Support

Many pastoral ministers have training and experience in bereavement counseling and support. Many FBOs also have bereavement support ministries and/or groups.

15. Exploring Issues of Meaning and Significance

Clergy and pastoral ministers may assist people in understanding the meaning and implications of significant life events, losses, and tragedies. This can be done in individual pastoral counseling, through group interventions, or in the context of the gathering of the faith community in various forums or in worship settings.

What Else Can Pastors Do?

According to Charles Kemp, "With kindness and understanding, with insight and skill, the clergy have led people to be better adjusted to life, while never losing sight of larger ideas."[2] Here is a list of other tasks not mentioned by Gunn above:

Being aware that guilt is often a problem among survivors—let them talk about it.

Be alert for problems related to increased smoking, alcoholism, drug abuse, suicide.

Be alert for people experiencing depression (especially 2–3 months following disaster).

Be alert for family problems as a result of the disaster (martial discord, delinquency).

Lutheran Disaster Response (LDR) has a helpful booklet for pastors for use in the aftermath of disasters.[3]

What Else Can Lay Members Do?

LDR also has a booklet for faith community members on how to help both members of their own congregation and people in the broader community.[4] Laypersons can offer whatever resources they have to the programs or initiatives in which their churches are involved. This may include providing for the basic needs of disaster survivors if EMS workers and other government agencies are not able to do so, or performing homemaker or yard services or offering financial support both immediately following the disaster and during long-term recovery. More than likely, however, rather than providing for basic survival needs, laypersons can offer their time and attention to victims who may be isolated, lonely, or grieving because of the losses brought on by the disaster. Many of the tasks described above for clergy may need to be carried out by the laity if clergy are not available.

Developing a Disaster Plan

Congregations need to prepare themselves before a disaster strikes to ensure the safety of their members and the intactness of their facilities. Lutheran Disaster Response has outlined what congregations need to know before, during, and after disasters strike. Below are practical steps that need to be taken and documented beforehand (this section has been taken largely verbatim from the LDR Web site[5] with some editing and elaboration).

Before a Disaster Strikes

1. Prepare the staff of the religious organization to be ready in case of disaster:

   (a) Assign someone to be responsible as the disaster-response coordinator and provide them with authority.
   (b) Identify alternative persons who can take over if that person in charge is unable to do their duties.
   (c) Be sure to establish a clear and explicit line of command so that there will be no question about who is in charge or has the authority to make decisions.
   (d) Prepare lay leaders to lead worship and teach Sunday school if the pastor is disabled or unavailable because of a disaster.
   (e) Be sure that all staff have training in first aid and cardiopulmonary resuscitation (CPR) for treating both youth and adults.
   (f) Train ushers to respond appropriately in case of fire or sudden collapse of a member of the congregation.
   (g) Train children's ministry staff to respond to emergencies or disasters.

2. Take a survey of your facilities, members, resources, and programs to identify special concerns during and following a disaster that need to be addressed and the resources available to address them.

3. Develop formal agreements on how and when to use your resources with the Red Cross, other emergency-management agencies, local mental health center/authority, and a faith-based social service organization (either within your denomination or outside of it).

4. Know your resources and identify their functions in the event of a disaster.

5. Develop a process for raising funds for disaster relief from within your congregation, and be aware of outside sources of funds from national faith-based groups or government agencies and how to acquire them rapidly.

6. Prepare your building/facility for disaster by developing a safety checklist:

(a) Have phones available in each area of the building and post emergency numbers by each phone (911, poison control center, police station, fire department); these phones should be accessible at all hours.

(b) Review insurance policies regularly, and keep copies in a safe deposit box at a local bank or off-site location, along with photographs and vital records.

(c) Find out where the nearest storm shelters are located and make this information readily available by contacting a single person designated with this information; alternative individuals should also be identified in case the responsible person cannot be reached.

(d) Post instructions in the entrance or foyer of the facility, clearly visible to all, about what to do and where to go in the event of a severe storm or tornado warning.

(e) Have a plan of evacuation in case of fire, and practice fire drills regularly.

(f) Ensure that there is a battery-operated radio in the office of the church and that someone is listening for severe storm watches if a function is going on in the facility during bad weather.

(g) Identify and train people (and be sure there are trained backups) to cut off the electricity, gas, and other utilities; place covers over windows; and secure materials inside and outside the building.

(h) Stockpile an adequate supply of emergency needs, including emergency lights, flashlights, batteries, first-aid kits, blankets, cots, canned foods, and water.

(i) Establish a prayer phone tree of people who will pray and if necessary give blood in the event of a disaster.

(j) Check to be sure that exits are clearly marked with lighted signs and are free of obstruction.

(k) Ensure that all locked doors have crash bars.

(l) All upper floors should have evacuation routes clearly designated, and there should be a special evacuation plan for handicapped people that does not rely on elevators run by electricity.

(m) Check all electrical equipment, including circuit breakers cover switches, outlet boxes, ground electrical units, and pay special attention not to overload the circuits.

(n) Know where the gas main and meter shut-off valve are located (and be sure that there is a gas wrench nearby to turn off the valve).

(o) Be sure that fire extinguishers are fully charged and up to date on inspections, and arrange to have extinguishers for different kinds of fires (electrical, grease, and regular).

(p) Be sure that all smoke detectors are working properly and that batteries are fully charged.

(q) Be sure that all paint, solvents, cleaning fluids, thinners, toners, propane, toxic or corrosive materials are stored properly.[6]

7. Prepare the members of the congregation to respond effectively to disaster:

(a) Encourage family disaster preparation (see Red Cross family preparation checklist).[7]

(b) Someone trained in CPR and first aid should be at every church function.

(c) Identify special procedures for evacuating the vision-impaired, hearing-impaired, physically disabled, and those with medical problems.

(d) Have a plan to check on the needs of congregation members after a disaster (i.e., have a follow-up plan), and be prepared to distribute food or meet other basic needs.

(e) Organize volunteer groups to help in time of disaster (develop such a list prior to a disaster), including an order of rotation to ensure that no one is overburdened.

8. Work with other churches to join forces and resources (in community-wide disasters):

(a) Set up reciprocal agreements with another church or churches to meet if the home church is damaged.

(b) Develop a coordinated plan with other local churches to meet the needs of the highly vulnerable in the community, such as those of advanced age, the disabled, large single-parent families, etc.

(c) Develop a plan to distribute hygiene supplies, baby supplies, food, water, and other basic necessities.

(d) Have regular meetings of religious leaders who make up ministerial associations or interfaith groups to discuss how congregations can work together in the event of a disaster.

(e) Prepare with other churches that are located a considerable distance away so that both you and they are unlikely to be affected by a single disaster; the unaffected congregation can then provide temporary housing, supplies, and volunteers to the affected one.

During and After a Disaster

When a disaster strikes, congregations need to be prepared to act immediately. Then, as the aftermath of the disaster begins to settle in, members need to be prepared to serve over the long hall.

1. Rescue/emergency phase:

(a) Survey church staff and members of congregation to determine immediate needs.

(b) Ensure that staff and members of congregation have adequate food, shelter, and energy (electricity and natural gas).

(c) Ensure that materials are on hand, such as dry ice, generators, and chain saws, to provide more advanced assistance.

(d) If possible, offer your church as temporary shelter and, if possible, first contact the Red Cross (since a Red Cross inspection may be required).

(e) Offer pastoral services to those in need if there are casualties (i.e., to family members, close friends, etc).

(f) As soon as the immediate basic needs of staff and members of the congregation are met, inspect church facilities for damage and make temporary repairs as necessary.

(g) Contact the denominational headquarters in your region and alert them to your needs and the resources you have to offer.

2. Relief phase:

(a) Assist with repairs and cleanup first for members of the congregation and then for others in the community affected (patching roofs, removing debris, cooking as necessary).

(b) Contact partners in your area, including other FBOs and the Red Cross, either to request assistance or to offer help.

(c) Mobilize volunteers from the congregation to serve at food centers, Red Cross shelters, and cleanup crews (ensure this is in coordination with other relief organizations).

(d) Provide a listening ear to those in need, both within and outside of the faith community.

(e) Discourage the spreading of unhelpful rumors.

(f) Help disaster victims apply for assistance.

(g) Take up a special offering to assist disaster victimss

(h) Inquire about matching funds from regional and national denominational offices, as well as from state and national organizations (SEMA, FEMA, etc.), especially funds for delivering mental health servicess

3. Recovery phase:

(a) Become involved in disaster response ministry to victims in your area.

(b) If not already done, connect with other FBOs in order to join resources and provide a coordinated response (coordination is crucial)

(c) Either hold or participate in a meeting of local religious leaders to develop a long-term recovery plan.

(d) Identify and address the mental and spiritual needs that become especially prominent after the shock of the disaster and immediate relief phases have passed (anger, grief, depression, anxiety, loneliness).

(e) Match resources (pastoral care, social and psychological support) with needs in the congregation and the outside community; avoid duplication of servicess

For a detailed outline on how to develop a comprehensive mental health disaster plan for a faith community, see the Resources section on pages 123–37.

Summary

There is much that pastors and members of the faith community need to know about preparing for and responding to disasters. Congregations need to be prepared to ensure that when disaster strikes they will be ready to meet the immediate physical needs of their staff, members, and facilities. If they are successful in meeting these basic needs and in rapidly repairing any damage done by the disaster to their facilities, then they will be free to meet the emotional, social, and spiritual needs of each other and of those in the surrounding community—needs that surface soon after physical needs are met. Rather than being the receivers of aid, congregations that have prepared for disaster will be those who lead the disaster response.

eight

Barriers and Obstacles to Integration

Numerous barriers prevent the faith community from becoming more involved in disaster preparation and response, especially in the area of mental health care. I discuss some of these below, dividing them into barriers that come from outside FBOs (i.e., government agencies, EMS workers, mental health counselors, etc.) and barriers that come from within the FBO itself. I conclude by addressing the biggest obstacle to integration, territoriality.

Barriers from the Outside

Lack of Information

One of the greatest barriers is lack of information by EMS personnel about the contributions that FBOs can make. A great deal of misinformation circulates as well. Many providers either don't realize that spiritual needs are important or think that others are addressing them adequately. The Red Cross, for example, while it has a spiritual team for responding to major emergencies, provides relatively little spiritual care to disaster victims in most locations, and Red Cross volunteers quickly leave the scene soon after the immediate needs of survivors are met. The Red Cross is usually gone when disaster victims move into short-term and long-term aftermath phases, the time when psychological and spiritual needs are greatest. As a result, such needs often fall through the cracks. In other instances, EMS workers think that large faith-based social service agencies are meetings these needs when they are not. For example, according to Rabbi Davidowitz-Farkas, the United Services Group in New York City did not think it necessary to include disaster spiritual care at its table because the group incorrectly believed that all religious needs were being addressed by Catholic Charities.

EMS groups are frequently unaware of what the faith community has to offer. There is the misconception that faith communities only help "their own," and do not feel an obligation to the broader community. This is usually not correct. Likewise, there is sometimes a misconception that the faith community becomes involved only to proselytize people at their weakest moments. While this may occur in some cases, most of the time, members of faith communities want to become involved because of their own personal faith and desire to relieve the suffering of others, not to convert them. Faith-based organizations such as Catholic Charities or Lutheran Social Services provide many social services and are often already involved on a governmental level since they are part of the overall response effort. These FBOs often have Memorandums of Understanding (MOU), either with a governmental agency or with its designee, such as the American Red Cross. For example, the Southern Baptist Men provide meals during disaster response. Their MOU states that they are not to preach or try to convert vulnerable disaster victims.

EMS groups need to understand that faith-based responders are often in disaster recovery for the long haul. They work with individuals and communities in mid- and long-term recovery. They are usually not the ones who send their clergy onto a site to provide disaster spiritual care during the first two weeks (although they may be involved in providing material resources for disaster relief during this time).

Excessive and Exclusive Focus on the Immediate Crisis

Most EMS groups get caught up in responding to the initial disaster, removing the offending agent, insuring safety of survivors, and meeting basic needs. Disaster response, however, is not only emergency response but also responding to victims as they attempt to put their lives back together. EMS agencies often forget that the community itself has resources that can sustain victims once the immediate disaster passes. Community resources, however, are seldom supported or even acknowledged as playing a role. Disaster funding should be put behind such community resources to sustain recovery over the long haul.

Failure to Address the Whole Person

Because of their focus on preserving life and meeting basic physical needs, EMS personnel can sometimes forget that disasters cause other wounds besides physical ones. These wounds often do not become evident until basic needs are met and victims begin to process what just happened to them, their families, their homes, jobs, and futures. Failure to address these other needs—psychological, social, and often spiritual—may leave many victims so impaired that they cannot go on with their lives, nullifying much of the good that was done by helping them to survive physically. Lack of recognition and assessment of such needs serves as a major barrier to valuing the role that faith communities can play in disaster response and limits their ability to meet such needs effectively.

Failure to Assess or Understand the Importance of Spiritual Needs

EMS personnel often feel inadequate in assessing spiritual/pastoral needs. Sometimes mental health counselors feel the same. When spiritual issues come up, they either ignore them or quickly hand people over to the clergy rather than seeing that both psychological and spiritual issues may need to be addressed simultaneously. Collaboration involves each profession understanding and valuing the importance of what the other has to offer and working together to meet the need. In the next chapter, I provide a brief assessment tool for assessing spiritual needs.

Failure to Understand the Need for Counseling during Long-term Recovery

Because EMS agencies, the Red Cross, and other disaster response organizations deal with only the immediate situation and then move on to address other emergencies, there is little understanding of what the needs of victims are in long-term recovery. Although considerable research has documented the persistence of psychological symptoms and disorders long after a disaster passes, little research has focused on the counseling needs of survivors six months, one year, or five years after an event—except for those with more severe disorders such as PTSD or major depression. Less obvious psychological wounds may result in divorce, substance abuse, or failure to find work or live productive lives, and these often go unnoticed. Even less is known about how "spiritual recovery" affects quality of life years after a disaster. If we knew more about how spiritual struggles impact human flourishing, perhaps there would be more value placed on spiritual care (by EMS workers, mental health counselors, and even by faith communities who sometimes don't recognize the important role they can play).

Belief That Only Professional Mental Health Care Is Needed

More than ten years after the Piper Alpha oil platform tragedy, Hull and colleagues assessed the mental health status of thirty-six of the original fifty-nine survivors.[1] Over 20 percent still met the most stringent diagnostic criteria for PTSD. When inquiring about sources of help, they found that nonprofessional support (from friends, family, faith community) was perceived as being the most helpful by far compared to benefits from medication or group therapy. Red Cross workers reported a similar response after the September 11 terrorist attacks, when survivors often preferred to talk with clergy rather than with mental health counselors,[2] a fact that was confirmed by a national survey of the population soon after 9/11.[3]

Based on interviews with forty-six acknowledged international experts on mental health and disaster management, Weiss and colleagues[4] stressed the importance of mental health policy following disasters that emphasized "(a) assessing the local socio-cultural setting, (b) relating this context to the local formulation of problems, and (c) identifying features of the culture and community that suggest local ways of coping." Thus, crisis counselors need to work with local community groups in addressing mental health problems following disasters. While they provide a critical role in addressing many serious psychological problems, mental health professionals need to recognize that addressing spiritual needs is an important part of whole person mental health care and special training is required to address them.

Competition between Mental Health Providers and FBOs

Another serious barrier to greater cooperation between FBOs and the local mental health authority is fear of competition. There is a long and ugly history between mental health professionals and the religious community.[5] Until recently, most religious people were believed by mental health professionals to be neurotic or unbalanced (see Freud's work). Furthermore, some mental health professionals saw the faith community as encroaching on their territory—clergy with limited training seeking to counsel and meet mental health needs. Writing about how pastoral counseling centers represent a threat to community mental health centers, one psychiatrist wrote: "Other non-medical professionals are also becoming involved in the delivery of mental health services. A large group of newcomers are ministers and rabbis. . . . The pastoral counseling movement may be looked upon as either an ally that reaches a population often untouched by psychiatrists or as a negative force attempting to usurp yet more of what was once psychiatrists' turf."[6] These territorial issues also exist in the disaster field.

Failure to Understand That Clergy Can Increase Access

Crisis counselors need to better understand the culture and mentality of the people they are serving. All the degrees and experience in the world won't necessarily get you in the door unless the people you are serving view themselves as needing you and view you as being potentially helpful.[7] Many disaster victims are members of faith communities and may be resistant to mental health care, which they may view as antireligious or not valuing the importance of faith (see "Stigma against Mental Health Care," page 104).

Even traumatized EMS personnel are often wary of accepting help from mental health professionals. For example, firefighters in New York City following 9/11 did not want to see "counselors." However, they were willing to meet with and discuss their needs with trained peers and clergy. Francis Gunn believes that his clergy group was instrumental in helping to break down the barriers that later enabled many FDNY members to take greater advantage of their Counseling Services Unit. Thus, clergy may actually help to pave the way for increased use of professional mental health services by victims and EMS workers. Cooperation and collaboration rather than competition with clergy, then, may actually benefit mental health professionals because of increased referrals.

Lack of Relationship

EMS personnel and crisis counselors are often wary of clergy coming in and doing things that they do not view as helpful. FBOs often lack the relationships with EMS groups that are necessary for integration into the emergency response system. Wanting to do good and help the suffering, FBOs may strike out on their own and in their own way to meet the needs that they see. These independent efforts can be very helpful in some circumstances, especially where EMS personnel are greatly understaffed; in other situations, however, FBOs can get in the way, contribute to confusion and disorganization, and lead to uneven distribution of services. A lot more dialogue needs to take place to engender trust and collaboration at the local level.

Barriers within FBOs

Lack of Training

Given the immensity of human suffering that follows disasters, clergy often struggle to meet the psychological, social, and spiritual needs of disaster victims. One reason for this is lack of training in disaster response. Rabbi Davidowitz-Farkas emphasizes that disaster ministry is very different from congregational ministry.[8] When responding to a disaster victim, the clergy's role is that of comforter rather than preacher, theologian, or evangelist, and primarily involves listening, validating, holding hands, and acknowledging the inadequacy of "pat" spiritual answers to questions of why and how. Clergy must also have knowledge about the cultural, ethnic, and religious diversity of the population they are serving so that spiritual support can be truly "person-centered."

Clergy also need training in basic skills such as active listening and validation, in coping strategies helpful to trauma victims, and in implementing effective spiritual interventions. Clergy need to learn about the phases of disaster such as the initial impact, early aftermath, short-term aftermath, and long-term aftermath phases described in chapter 1. This will help them to implement the most appropriate, timely, and effective interventions. Clergy must be able to distinguish normal responses to trauma from complicated grief and extreme reactions to stress so that they can refer such individuals for professional mental health care. Finally, as emphasized repeatedly, clergy must be organized and their activities integrated into other disaster response efforts.

Pastor and clinical psychologist Andrew Weaver points out that there is only limited up-to-date mental health information written specifically for parish-based clergy on what kinds of help disaster survivors need and how to provide that help.[9] He observes that the almost total absence of research on clergy addressing the emotional and spiritual needs of disaster victims has further marginalized them from the formal mental health network. In response to this need for more information, Weaver and colleagues have written a book entitled *Counseling Survivors of Traumatic Events: A Handbook for Pastors and Other Helping Professionals*.[10] Within it, they outline what clergy and faith communities can do to meet the whole person needs of trauma victims. It provides case vignettes of clergypersons counseling trauma victims; gives crisis-specific recommendations on helpful clergy responses, as well as guidelines on self-care for religious professionals who counsel trauma victims and are often vulnerable themselves to post-traumatic stress.

Lack of Information about How the Disaster Response System Works

When a disaster strikes, people within the faith community feel compelled to help. They have been taught to be responsible for meeting the needs of others. As a result, they want to do something to relieve the suffering of those affected by disasters, whether local or distant. Teams of church members and resources may be mobilized. These teams may travel to the area where the disaster has occurred. Rather than be welcomed with open arms by EMS workers, they may be rebuffed and prevented from helping. Lack of information on how the disaster response system works and failure to be aware of the need to integrate their response with efforts by others can create frustration on all sides.

Lack of Local Coordination of FBOs

With so many different faith-based groups wishing to provide support and other mental health services to disaster victims, in addition to the secular agencies providing such services, there is considerable potential for conflict and duplication of services. This depends to a substantial degree on the availability of secular mental health services, which may vary widely depending on disaster locale and extent. Currently, there is no commonly used system to triage well-meaning volunteers from the faith community based on their qualifications and credentials. As noted above, EMS workers may resist help offered by members of the faith community for fear that they will get in the way or cause more harm than good. Devising a system to integrate and coordinate the efforts of faith-based organizations would go a long way to streamline the process, reduce resistances, and carve out a recognized place in the emergency response system where faith community involvement will be welcome and encouraged.

Stigma against Mental Health Care

There is often a stigma against mental health services among religious persons—that is, survivors should be able to pray their way out of their horrible circumstances, relying on God or the faith community instead of secular resources of support and healing. However, experience shows that many disaster victims require both kinds of support to get their lives back together. Education is needed to counteract unhelpful religious attitudes that prevent victims from working with mental health professionals when they need such help.

Resistance to Collaborating with Other Faith Communities

Faith communities are accustomed to serving the needs of their own members and others according to their own tradition of compassion and social service. Some may not want to "dilute" their mission by being part of an interfaith or interdisciplinary approach. The result is isolation and lack of partnerships with other local faith communities that prevent a coordinated, unified response.

Differences in Theology

There can be significant differences in the views of various faith communities about how God works in people's lives. There are also many differing views on the relationship of life events to the concept of God's will or God's plan for people, causing conflict on how spiritual issues ought to be addressed. Spiritual needs may be viewed differently as well.

More broadly, what does the term "faith-based organization" really mean? According to Rabbi Zahara Davidowitz-Farkas, this is a troublesome sticking point. Is an FBO defined as a large, religiously affiliated social service agency such as Lutheran Disaster Response, Catholic Charities, or Episcopal Relief? Is it local mainline churches and clergy? What about the myriad of "independent" or nondenominational churches, which are probably the ones whose clergy have the greatest power in their individual congregations? What about the Jewish community, which is structured and responds very differently than its Christian counterparts? What about the Muslim or Buddhist communities, which have never before been part of this conversation? And there are others. These groups are usually lumped together, but they need to be approached idiosyncratically. Each requires a different approach. One size cannot fit all. This represents a major challenge when trying to coordinate the faith-based response.

The Greatest Obstacle

Of all barriers, territoriality is the greatest. Besides competition between crisis counselors and religious professionals providing mental health services, FBOs among themselves are often quite sensitive about who "gets the credit" for making a difference. Thus, they encounter some of the same "political" challenges that all human organizations face. This leads to competition and conflict, rather than collaboration and cooperation in meeting people's needs.

Rabbi Davidowitz-Farkas emphasizes the extent of the politics within the religious disaster response community in New York City. She provides some rather eye-opening observations from her perspective:

Everyone is jockeying for position. Disaster response is now a sexy thing and everyone wants to be seen at "the pit." One of the problems is that religious groups are preparing as if every disaster is a 9/11. This appears to be happening within New York City. One small example of this is that large apartment building fires are not "valued" as much as the ferry accident was.

The problems are generated by politics, territoriality, and the overreach of MOU [memorandum of understanding] guidelines. This is especially evident in the relationship between FBOs and the American Red Cross. ARC, for example, is responsible for providing health and mental health services. These are federally mandated responsibilities. ARC also became responsible for making sure that appropriate spiritual care is provided. Among other things, the government was careful to give this responsibility to a group who in its mission is not sectarian and is inclusive by definition. Faith-based disaster responders, however, feel cheated and think that, since they are in the business of religion, they should be the ones providing this service. Their MOUs, however, specifically do not speak about the provision of religious care, but only about basic support needs such as food, clothing, and shelter."[11]

Francis Gunn agrees that the greatest obstacle that he has found that prevents emergency, mental health, and pastoral professionals from working together is territoriality. This issue has impaired the cooperation of various organizations doing disaster work over the past twelve years that he has been involved. High-profile disasters and critical incidents provide opportunities for emergency services, mental health providers, and pastoral professionals to "shine." Many helping professionals are naturally drawn to these incidents, which make for powerful helping and healing stories. They truly appeal to the instinctive desire of these professionals to "make a difference." Thorough pre-planning, good training, and an inclusive approach that respects the unique contributions of all the various professional groups and the valuable role of trained volunteers will go a long way toward breaking down territoriality and overcoming the "every man for himself" approach when responding to disaster.

There are many parallels between the emergence of disaster mental health care as a field and the growing recognition of spiritual care as a discipline. The field of disaster mental health began with the work of

Gerard Jacobs from the Disaster Mental Health Institute at the University of South Dakota and Jane Morgan of the American Red Cross.[12] This happened about fifteen years ago after Jacobs was asked to respond to a plane crash. At that time, there was a lot of resistance to the idea of disaster mental health. Aside from a general wariness about mental health, Health Services considered itself the mental health provider and didn't want this newcomer to encroach on its territory. Much the same has been happening with mental health and spiritual care, although much effort is being made to build trust and work in an interdisciplinary fashion. Many say that spiritual care is in the same place now that mental health care was fifteen years ago.

Summary

Despite the great need for integration and cooperation between EMS services, crisis counselors, and faith-based disaster response groups, many barriers to this currently exist. Lack of information and education, lack of relationship and planning beforehand, lack of trust on both sides, and territoriality between these groups (and within the faith community) are the greatest barriers to supporting, expanding, and including FBOs in disaster response. Considerable effort and specific steps by all sides are needed to help overcome these barriers to a unified community response.

nine

Overcoming the Barriers

On the one hand, how might the government and EMS groups in charge of national and local disaster response best engage FBOs in planning and outreach? What can they do to support FBO efforts in disaster planning and response? In what ways might the role of FBOs in disaster response be expanded beyond what is currently happening, emphasizing the unique resources that faith-based groups have to offer? On the other hand, how might faith communities overcome many of the internal barriers that prevent them from being more effective in the disaster response effort? I provide recommendations for EMS groups and faith communities below.

Recommendations for EMS groups

Here are steps that EMS groups and crisis counselors can take to learn more about the spiritual needs of disaster victims and support greater FBO involvement:

Research

Research is needed to determine the prevalence of spiritual needs and the extent to which they are met (and by whom) during each phase of a disaster. Further research on the relationship between addressing spiritual needs (or failure to address them) and long-term mental health following disasters is critical. Systematic data are needed on the involvement and activities of clergy and lay volunteers from the faith community following disasters. Additional systematic information is also needed on the barriers described in chapter 8 in order to document them and provide strategies to overcoming them. This includes information on conflict at the local level between EMS personnel, crisis counselors, clergy, and lay volunteers.

Education

Although more research is clearly needed, much is already known that justifies a major educational initiative directed toward EMS agencies/ personnel, mental health authorities, and FBOs to help dispel myths and misconceptions, to define the unique roles that each group serves, and to emphasize the consequences of not valuing and including each other in disaster response. Each group needs an education program tailored to its specific needs that address the barriers described in the previous chapter.

More specifically, EMS agencies (FEMA, SEMA, local EMS responders, the Red Cross, etc.) and mental health authorities (SMHA, county mental health clinics, crisis counselors, etc.) need to learn about the resources that FBOs can provide when disasters strike. Religious beliefs and practices are usually associated with better mental health and improved coping with stress.[1] Religious or spiritual interventions result in faster recovery from emotional disorders such as anxiety and depression, especially in religious persons. Spiritual needs, particularly those related to meaning and purpose and understanding God's role, are widespread during the short-term and long-term aftermath phases of disasters. The extent to which these spiritual needs are met by the emergency response system now in place is largely unknown.

Assessment

EMS agencies and mental health authorities need to train their front-line personnel to include spiritual/pastoral needs as part of their needs assessment in working with victims of disaster. Many EMS personnel will not be comfortable doing this, given their lack of expertise. However, a few simple questions can be asked that will identify spiritual needs that can then be referred to trained spiritual caregivers to address. The types of questions asked as part of such an assessment might include the following:

- Are religious or spiritual beliefs important to you?
- Are your religious or spiritual beliefs a source of comfort or a source of stress now?

- In what way are they comforting or stressful?
- Are you a member of a religious or spiritual community and is it supportive?
- Do you have any spiritual struggles or needs that you would like help with?

Leadership

EMS agencies should take the lead in inviting FBOs to participate. Government agencies should encourage interested FBOs to identify the types of resources they wish to contribute to the disaster response effort. This may range from efforts to coordinate disaster response; mobilize and train clergy and lay volunteers to provide psychological, social, and spiritual support; raise funds or material necessities to assist victims during their recovery; or many other potential activities described in this book. Government agencies need to work with FBOs to determine what type of collaboration at the national, state, county, and local community level might be most helpful, and then actively enroll FBO leaders and representatives to participate during the planning, pre-disaster phase. In many cases the most practical and efficient response will be to establish collaborative plans and efforts between local FBOs and local EMS agencies, since this is often where most of the action occurs. In order to ensure uniformity and basic standards in response, such local activity will probably need to be coordinated at the state or national level.

Also, government and EMS agencies need to encourage mental health authorities to be proactive, rather than resistive or obstructive, in their relationships with FBOs. Mental health authority leaders could become members of voluntary associations that typically include the major faith-based groups (such as NVOAD or a state VOAD). Again, by participating in such meetings, plans can be made on how to better work together with faith groups, recognizing and utilizing their strengths and unique gifts.

Include FBOs in Planning

On the local level, EMS agencies should include mobilization of FBOs as part of their response protocol. As indicated above, this will require that leadership from the local FBOs be included in disaster response planning. Both Father Francis Gunn and Rabbi Davidowitz-Farkas emphasize that clergy should become integrated into local, state, and federal disaster response protocols during the planning stage—not after a disaster occurs. Representatives from FBOs should be included in disaster planning and response at the highest levels (FEMA, Red Cross, etc.) and at regional levels as well (SEMA, SMHA, etc.). FEMA and SEMA, in turn, could encourage police, fire departments, and other local EMS personnel to include FBOs in disaster planning and response.

Encourage Teamwork, Partnership, and Collaboration

The "every man for himself" approach, as discussed earlier and emphasized repeatedly in this report, is one of the first attitudinal barriers that needs to be overcome. In New York City following the World Trade Center attacks, hundreds of crisis counselors, other mental health professionals, and many clergy were "turned away" or frustrated in their attempts to help. Francis Gunn saw this firsthand in his work with the New York City Fire Department, which maintained very tight control over who could come to the aid of the firefighters impacted by the disaster.

Partnerships should be encouraged between crisis counselors and local faith-based groups. Mental health workers should be encouraged to visit or participate with local ministerial associations or church councils. In this way, the two groups could develop working relationships before a disaster strikes. Some cities, such as Chicago, have religious associations with representatives from all of the major religious groups in the city. Participation in such associations by mental health representatives, even if only to familiarize themselves with the work of these groups, is recommended. When disasters strike, such relationships and partnerships with FBOs will serve as important channels for delivering services.

Encourage Bidirectional Referral Networks before Disasters Occur

Mental health counselors could offer a spiritual component by developing a referral network with local pastoral counselors or clergy. Faith-based groups, in turn, could refer members who need specialized mental health care to these mental health counselors. Furthermore, mental health counselors could provide education to faith-based communities on how to identify mental disorders, which kinds of interventions might be helpful, and when to refer. For example, mental health professionals can teach a Sunday school class on managing grief, or could even consider holding a clinic in a large religious congregation, coming out once or twice a week to provide services at the church. These kinds of interactions will help to establish referral patterns before a disaster and will ensure that relationships are sufficiently developed so that they can be immediately activated when a disaster strikes. Unfortunately, interactions between mental health authorities and religious communities have historically been either nonexistent or competitive and antagonistic (as discussed above). These barriers need to come down for the good and the security of the community. Government agencies should support and provide incentives for such cooperation and relationship building.

Consider Making Trained Clergy First Responders in Mental Health Care

FBOs are present in every community and two-thirds of Americans are members of faith communities. Besides offering necessary spiritual support, local clergy are ideally positioned to serve as "first responders" in meeting the psychological needs of disaster victims. In many communities, clergy serve this function anyway following disasters. However, making this part of the formal EMS response would help to systematize and coordinate the effort. Interested clergy would need to be identified beforehand and volunteer for special training in order to serve in this role (like chaplains).

Since only a proportion of disaster victims need formal mental health services, and since those services may be of limited availability, local clergy could provide support to those who only need support and triage those with more complex needs to mental health professionals—enhancing the efficiency with which scarce specialized mental health services are utilized. This would also increase the likelihood that people would accept mental health services, if referred by trusted clergy. It would result in a better matching of need with scarce mental health resources. For example, when

Francis Gunn and his colleagues were asked to respond to the needs of fire-fighters and their families following the World Trade Center attacks, they designed an interdisciplinary approach using trained firefighter peers and trained clergy to do the initial assessments in the firehouses. The trained peers and clergy then acted as contact points for referral to the mental health Counseling Services Unit (CSU) or for getting the CSU to deliver services in locations with the greatest need.

Protection

Emergency management agencies need to have mechanisms in place to provide FBO responders with debriefing and other methods of protection from burnout and vicarious stress. Father Gunn, Rabbi Davidowitz-Farkas, and Dr. Weaver all emphasize the need for clergy who respond to disasters to practice good self-care and network with other individuals who can provide support. Again, helping clergy to establish such networks, identify colleagues, and develop a support system before a disaster occurs will ensure that such networks are in place when they are needed.

Funding

First, greater flexibility is needed in the support options that the Substance Abuse and Mental Health Services Administration (SAMHSA) now offers. These options should address the pastoral care needs of disaster victims during short-term and possibly long-term recovery. It is during recovery, as people begin to put their lives back together, that issues of meaning and purpose in life begin to surface and pastoral care services are most needed. Disaster-trained pastoral counselors or chaplains are clergy most suited for this role. These individuals have both a degree in ministry from a three-year seminary and a master's or doctorate degree in counseling, which membership in the American Association of Pastoral Counselors requires. Members of the Association of Professional Chaplains have similar training.

Grants are now given to local mental health authorities to respond to disasters. There needs to be a mechanism in place so that some of this support can go toward pastoral counseling or frontline clergy screening. This may be tricky to orchestrate in order to avoid competition between pastoral groups and local mental health authorities, which could adversely affect the development of the partnerships so critical to these groups. Thus, the funding mechanisms for local mental health and pastoral organizations should probably be separate from one another.

Second, the application process for available funding needs to be made easier. According to the Robert T. Stafford Disaster Relief and Emergency Assistance Act, Section 416, Public Law 100-707, SAMHSA is authorized to give grants to "local non-profit agencies" to provide short-term mental health services in presidentially declared disaster areas.[2] These nonprofit agencies must be "recommended by the Governor and accepted by the Secretary." Workshops could be offered by SAMHSA to help educate FBOs [nonprofit agencies] on how to apply for such federal funds. At a minimum, FBOs should be given the same opportunity to compete for such funds as other community nonprofits. Efforts should also be made to educate state governors about the role and availability of FBOs to provide such services so that they won't be surprised when approached with such requests.

Recommendations for Faith Communities

Here are specific steps that faith communities can take to increase their involvement, integration, and impact during and following disasters.

Recognize the Powerful Role That Faith Can Play

Disasters create tremendous anxiety, grief, and isolation. They also give rise to many theological questions and spiritual needs. Personal religious faith can help to meet these psychological, social, and spiritual needs. Members of faith communities need to acknowledge and utilize their faith as a powerful healing tool. This may seem self-evident, but many of those in the religious community do not realize that scientific research exists that documents the healing power of religious beliefs and practices.[3] Religious faith should also motivate members of congregations to become involved in helping their neighbors who are suffering. In particular, those in the faith community who are disaster victims should force themselves to become active in helping other survivors cope with their losses. It is through this joint effort of people helping each other that individuals and communities truly heal and bond together.

Obtain Necessary Education and Training

FBO members need to obtain training on how and when to respond to the needs of disaster victims. Besides pastoral counselors and chaplains, community clergy and lay volunteers should seek education on how to address spiritual needs, provide psychological care, and offer social support, and when to refer victims for specialized services. Those who receive such training should be credentialed, and a streamlined system of notification and mobilization should be developed and adhered to by EMS groups. This might include the establishment of an FBO disaster network, which could help educate members of local faith communities on how they can participate and contribute to the disaster effort.

There are also formal programs of disaster response training that clergy and lay leaders can take in order to prepare them to act when needed. For example, Chaplain Dininger of Ormond Beach, Florida, obtained his disaster planning and response preparation by attending a course on Critical Incident Stress Management in Orlando held by Bob Vanderpol of the International Critical Incident Stress Foundation.[4] The American Association of Christian Counselors (AACC) sponsored the training. After obtaining this training, Dininger brought together a disaster response team based at the Ormond Beach hospital consisting of a psychologist, a nurse, and several area clergy. Many similar disaster training programs now exist for clergy and other spiritual caregivers.

Establish Relationships, Partnerships, and Collaboration

Faith communities need to learn how to establish relationships, organize, cooperate, and fit into the existing emergence response system, and to do so before disasters strike. Just as EMS workers and mental health professionals should initiate relationship with FBOs, FBOs should also make efforts to communicate with local EMS, mental health, and public health authorities. They should introduce themselves to these secular groups and describe to them what they have to offer and, in turn, find out what kinds of services these groups have to offer.

FBOs should also find out who their neighbors are in the faith community who have similar interests in disaster preparation and response. This includes other voluntary organizations active during disasters. For example, on the national level, the relief arms of several major denominations (Lutheran Disaster Relief, Catholic Charities, and Jewish Family Services) work closely together; similar cooperative efforts should be established at the local level. The key is to establish and nurture partnerships within the community before a disaster occurs to enhance community readiness.

Counteract Stigma against Mental Health Services

Leaders of faith-based organizations should seek to learn about and inform their congregations about the unique and important resources that mental health professionals can provide following disasters and during non-disaster periods. Helping members to recognize and value the importance of such services will help to foster a more cooperative atmosphere and lay the groundwork for effective partnerships when they are needed.

Organize and Coordinate

Given the territoriality and competition that exists among FBOs, an outside organization (established and empowered by some central EMS agency like FEMA, but led by members of the faith community) should coordinate FBO efforts. Once established, this "FBO Coordinating Group" could organize itself into national and local networks. Although several FBO coordinating groups exist today, they are not inclusive of all major religious groups and there is considerable competition between them. NVOAD includes other voluntary organizations and therefore is not strictly faith based. Furthermore, it and other coordinating groups, such as Church World Service, may have political and territorial issues that could be difficult to overcome.[5] Consequently, it may be more expedient to create an entirely new body focused on coordinating the faith-based effort. Most importantly, it would have the government's authority behind it.

This FBO Coordinating Group could have representatives from each of the interested religious denominations (and nondenominational groups) and receive FEMA assistance for disaster planning and response efforts. Each denominational representative of the national FBO Coordinating

Group could be a full-time position funded in part by FEMA and in part by the FBO. That person's job would be to ensure that disaster planning takes place at the local level by motivating, encouraging, and training regional denominational groups in disaster planning and response (i.e., perhaps at the presbytery, conference, or other regional level). That regional group, then, could encourage, train and provide educational resources to local congregations to involve them in disaster planning and prepare them for a coordinated disaster response.

Coordinate at the Local Level

Someone needs to be identified who will coordinate the local FBO response when regional FBO representatives or local EMS agencies request services. In small to mid-size towns (10,000–50,000), this might be the local hospital chaplain. In larger communities, it could be the fire department or police department chaplain or head of a local clergy group or ministerial association. Once set up, there should be a method of quickly communicating requests by EMS for needed services to this local FBO coordinating person, who can then mobilize FBOs in the area.

Seek Credentialing

Based on Francis Gunn's experience with September 11, and since that event, there is still no system for "credentialing" clergy or lay responders to determine who is qualified to provide services. Similarly, seven years after the Oklahoma City bombing, city leaders pointed out that it was important to develop a process of credentialing clergy in order to identify those who were properly trained.[6] Churches have widely different ways of credentialing clergy, ranging from the self-ordained to those who are highly trained. There needs to be a way of screening clergy and lay volunteers before sending them out into the field. Basic national standards should be established for credentialing (perhaps by the national FBO Coordinating Group referred to above). Methods of identifying persons credentialed in disaster response should be established prior to the next major disaster. The hours, days, and weeks after a disaster are not the time for the credentialing process; it needs to be done as part of pre-disaster planning for all those involved in disaster response, but especially for clergy, pastoral ministers, and lay volunteers. The Red Cross has already established some standards for credentialing that could be modified as appropriate. However, none of this will matter unless clergy and members of the faith community make the necessary efforts to obtain such credentials.

Summary

Although the barriers to integration of FBOs into the formal disaster response system are formidable, there are specific steps that can be taken to overcome these barriers. Attitudes of EMS groups and FBOs toward each other will need to be changed, education and training obtained by both sides, and careful integration and coordination of response planned before disasters occur. Considerable effort, creativity, and flexibility will be needed to accomplish this task. However, when major disasters occur—like what happened in New York City on September 11, 2001, and in New Orleans on August 29, 2005—we will be glad that emergency management services and faith communities have laid the necessary groundwork for a unified and coordinated response.

ten

Final Comments

The services provided by faith communities are material, psychological, and spiritual in nature and especially important during long-term recovery after other EMS agencies have left the scene. The faith community's role goes way beyond providing for the immediate physical needs of disaster victims. Unfortunately, faith leaders may not have the appropriate training to assess the psychological and spiritual consequences of severe traumatic stress and often do not have a robust network of contacts that enable them to make appropriate referrals when complex situations arise. I hope this book will help to inform, support, and guide faith communities to effectively integrate their unique contributions into the existing disaster planning and response structures. If faith communities are prepared and equipped to meet not only the material needs of trauma victims but also their spiritual and emotional needs, this will strengthen the readiness and resiliency of our communities in the face of disasters.

Besides being a resource for faith communities, this book should help public policy makers and emergency management groups become more familiar with the resources offered by faith communities and help them feel more comfortable working with FBOs during disasters. This will help to speed the work of disaster relief and lead to a more coordinated emergency response system. Recommendations are made here on specific steps that government and EMS groups can take to support faith-based efforts in disaster planning and response, and how to overcome the substantial barriers that currently exist.

Mental health professionals and crisis counselors often struggle with the role that religious professionals and lay volunteers play in helping victims of disasters. Religious and mental health professionals each serve unique and necessary roles in disaster response: religious profession- als helping with personal problems, relationship difficulties, and spiritual needs, as well as mental health professionals treating the emotional and mental disorders that often accompany traumatic events. These distinct roles utilize the strengths and training that each profession has to offer. Because of decades of separation and competition, however, religious and mental health professionals are often at odds. The result is confusion, frus- tration, overlapping care services (leading to conflict and competition), and gaps in care where large segments of the affected population receive no care at all because of lack of coordination of services. Thus, this book will help both mental health providers and faith communities to become better prepared to respond to disasters in ways that complement each oth- er's efforts rather than duplicate or compete with them.

There are a number of concrete steps that FBOs can take to expand their involvement in the mental health disaster response. It will require an initial involvement of time and resources in planning, as well as initiative and leadership. However, the long-term payoff is likely to be substantial in terms of improving the resiliency of their congregations and communities. Disasters already take a huge toll every year in this country, costing hun- dreds of billions of dollars and affecting millions of human lives, and may cost even more in the future, depending on our success in combating ter- rorism. Nearly 200,000,000 Americans are members of faith communities that are led by nearly 400,000 clergy. FBOs operate on theological teach- ings that emphasize "help thy neighbor." When disaster strikes, there are many neighbors to help. Studies show that when a spiritually motivated person helps a neighbor in need, *both* persons benefit in terms of better mental and even better physical health.[1] Faith communities are ideally po- sitioned to meet the spiritual and emotional needs of disaster victims and represent a largely underutilized, cost-effective army of volunteers. Howev- er, FBOs often lack the necessary direction, coordination, and training to make their efforts successful. Now is the time for FBOs to obtain the tools needed to become part of our country's standard response to natural disas- ters and acts of terrorism, and for the current emergency response system to welcome them on board.

Resources

In this section, I describe and provide contact information for disaster-related organizations, list disaster-related periodicals on mental health, describe funding sources for disaster mental health care, provide resources on disasters specific for faith communities (Web sites and periodicals focusing on mental health and coping), outline a comprehensive health disaster plan for faith communities, and list research studies on the role of faith and faith communities in disasters.

General Resources

Government, State, and Local

The five major organizations involved in disaster response, outside of the local fire and police departments, are:

1. Federal Emergency Management Agency (FEMA). FEMA provides funds through SAMHSA (see below) to pay for *short-term* local mental health services in *presidentially declared* disaster areas. Disaster victims are encouraged to inquire about this service when registering for disaster assistance. FEMA also has a toll-free helpline (1-800-621-FEMA) that can be called to find out where services can be obtained. Crisis counselors are also available on site at the Disaster Recovery Centers established in or close to the community affected by the disaster. FEMA points out that counseling services may also be available through the "American Red Cross, the Salvation Army, other voluntary agencies, as well as *places of worship*." See http://www.fema.gov/rrr/counsel.shtm.

2. Substance Abuse and Mental Health Services Administration (SAMHSA). In the Department of Health and Human Services, SAMHSA works closely with FEMA to provide mental health information to victims of disasters through the National Mental Health Information Center (800-789-2647) (see http://www.mentalhealth.org/cmhs/). SAMHSA also has a Disaster Technical Assistance Center (DTAC) that can be reached at 800-308-3515. Finally, SAMHSA has an Emergency Mental Health and Traumatic Stress Services Branch, which is responsible for assessing, promoting, and enhancing the resilience of Americans in times of disaster by offering grants for counseling outreach and for the training of crisis counselors to provide assistance after FEMA relief workers leave an area. See http://www.mentalhealth.org/publications/allpubs/KEN95-0011/default.asp

3. State Emergency Management Agency (SEMA). Information on whom to contact to get in touch with your local state SEMA can be obtained at http://www.fema.gov/fema/statedr.shtm. The mental health authority responsible for disaster mental health in your area may be listed.

4. American Red Cross. Individuals desiring counseling to deal with the aftermath of a disaster may also call a local branch of the American Red Cross (ARC). Although I could not find a specific arm or continuing program of the Red Cross that provides mental health services on the ARC Web site, the organization appear to provide mental health services depending on the specific disaster. For example, the Federal Response Plan for Aviation Disasters designates the American Red Cross as the lead agency to provide mental health services to victims of air disasters, family members, and rescue workers following disasters such as September 11. Consequently, the American Red Cross, The September 11th Fund, and the Mental Health Association of New York City conducted a collaborative outreach effort to provide victims of 9/11 with financial assistance for confidential mental health and substance abuse treatment. To contact the ARC national office, call 202-639-3520. To locate your local Red Cross office, see http://www.redcross.org/.

5. State Mental Health Association, State Division of Mental Health, Community Mental Health Center, or County Mental Health Center. Disaster victims may call these state and county agencies for questions about counseling services. Contact information for state mental health agencies can be located at http://www.ncd.gov/resources/mental.htm.

Other Federal and Private Agencies (see also Chapter 2)

Centers for Disease Control and Prevention. www.cdc.gov, 888-246-2675

National Center for Post-Traumatic Stress Disorder.
www.ncptsd.org, 802-296-6300

The National Child Traumatic Stress Network. www.nctsnet.org

National Emergency Management Association.
www.nemaweb.org/index.cfm, 859-244-8000

Disaster Mental Health Institute of the University of South Dakota. This institute, directed by Gerard A. Jacobs, one of the founders of disaster mental health, offers a Ph.D. track in disaster psychology and a graduate certificate in disaster mental health to licensed mental health professionals and graduate students in mental health. See http://www.usd.edu/dmhi/. Addressing spirituality is not part of the designated program, but Rabbi Zahara says that Jacobs is open to including a spiritual component.

Mental Health Resources
Periodicals

After a Disaster: Self-Care Tips for Dealing with Stress. This fact sheet provides suggestions for victims on how to help themselves cope with disasters. It is available at http://www.mentalhealth.org/publications/allpubs/KEN-01-0097/default. asp.

Disaster Counseling. This fact sheet provides suggestions on how to counsel disaster victims. See http://www.mentalhealth.org/publications/allpubs/KEN-01-0096/default.asp.

After a Disaster: A Guide for Parents and Teachers. This brochure provides suggestions for parents and teachers to help them counsel children. See http://www.mentalhealth.org/publications/allpubs/KEN-01-0093/default.asp. Also see *Age-specific Interventions at Home for Children in Trauma: From Preschool to Adolescence,* a fact sheet that can be obtained from http://www.mentalhealth.org/publications/allpubs/NMH02-0138/default.asp.

Psychosocial Issues for Older Adults in Disasters. This booklet contains information on how to provide support for older adult survivors of disasters. It discusses what makes older adults more vulnerable to disasters, the nature of disasters and responses to them, and provides a list of resources. See ftp://ftp.health.org/pub/ken/pdf/SMA99-3323/99-821.pdf.

Responding to the Needs of People with Serious and Persistent Mental Illness in Times of Major Disasters. This booklet provides a brief guide for mental health agency administrators, program planners, and providers of direct services to help them meet the disaster-related mental health needs of people with chronic mental illness who may require specialized strategies for accessing services. See http://www.mentalhealth.org/publications/allpubs/SMA96-3077/default.asp.

Disaster Mental Health: Crisis Counseling Programs for the Rural Community. This online booklet provides information about crisis counseling specifically for rural populations following disasters, taking into account the uniqueness of rural populations and how those factors affect the implementation of crisis counseling service. See http://www.mentalhealth.org/publications/allpubs/sma99-3378/crisiscounseling_fwd.asp.

Stress Prevention and Management Approaches for Rescue Workers in the Aftermath of Terrorist Acts. This fact sheet provides information on counseling and a hotline to call for emergency personnel on recovering from working at the site of terrorist acts. See http://www.mentalhealth.org/publications/allpubs/KEN01-0112/default.asp.

Field Manual for Mental Health and Human Service Workers in Major Disasters. This online booklet, intended for mental health workers and other human service providers, seeks to help those trying to help disaster survivors. It provides the basics of disaster mental health. See http://www.mentalhealth.org/publications/allpubs/ADM90-537/Default.asp.

Training Manual for Mental Health and Human Service Workers in Major Disasters. This online pamphlet, intended for instructors, describes effective interventions for responding to disaster stress and strategies for stress prevention and management among mental health and human service workers. See http://www.mentalhealth.org/publications/allpubs/ADM90-538/Default.asp.

Mental Health All-Hazards Disaster Planning Guidance. This online booklet is intended for state mental health associations and local mental health authorities to help them in disaster planning and response. However, it may also be useful for FBOs, since many of the same issues facing mental health authorities are those that FBOs must grapple when attempting to deliver mental health services. See http://www.mentalhealth.org/publications/allpubs/SMA03-3829/default.asp.

Funding for Mental Health Services

SAMHSA is authorized to provide supplemental emergency mental health counseling to individuals affected by major disasters, including the training of workers to provide such counseling. It does so through FEMA by providing funds for staff, travel, consultants, and other expenses for *short-term* mental health counseling and referral for "eligible survivors of Presidentially-declared major disasters."[1] These go to state or local nonprofit agencies as recommended by the state governor and accepted by the Secretary of the Department of Health and Human Services.[2]

Faith Community Resources

Web Sites

Disaster Response Web sites of Religious Denominations and Coordinating Groups. See chapter 6.

Best *national* sites are:

Church World Service Emergency Response Program.
http://www.cwserp.org/

Lutheran Disaster Response. http://www.ldr.org/

Evangelical Lutheran Church of American Disaster Response.
http://www.elca.org/dcs/disaster/

National Volunteer Organizations Active in Disasters.
http://www.nvoad.org/

Best *state* sites are:

North Carolina Interfaith Disaster Response. http://www.ncidr.org/

Florida Interfaith Networking in Disaster. http://www.floridadisasters.org/

Additional sites are:

Duke University's Center for the Study of Religion/Spirituality and Health. This Web site contains summaries of 2,500 studies and articles on religion, spirituality, and health, including over 1,000 studies on topics of mental health. Books, links to similar Web sites, and research training opportunities in religion and health are provided. The site serves as a portal of entry into the religion, mental health, and physical health research field. See http://www.dukespiritualityandhealth.org/.

Science & Theology News. A 36-page monthly newspaper with the latest news on research in science, religion, mental health, and health outcomes. Search the archives for articles on religion, spirituality, and disaster response. See http://www.stnews.org/.

HealthCare Chaplaincy. HCC is a chaplain training and research center located in heart of New York City. Disaster expert Andrew Weaver is the director of research at the institution. Contact Dr. Weaver to obtain information on chaplains involved in disaster training. See http://www.healthcarechaplaincy.org/.

Institute for Disaster Spiritual Care. Directed by Rabbi Zahara Davidowtiz-Farkas and located at 150 Amsterdam Avenue, New York, N.Y. This group of seventeen Jewish chaplains organized following September 11 and responded within minutes of the ferry disaster in New York City. For an article on the institute, see http://www.totallyjewish.com/news/stories/?disp_type=1&disp_story=kKTYdF.

Periodicals

Several denominational periodicals address counseling persons following disasters and talking about disasters with children. These can be found in chapter 5 under each denomination's disaster response Web site. An example includes the particularly detailed resource list on the Lutheran Disaster Response Web site; see http://www.ldr.org/CoordinatorResource.html.

Spiritual Care Bringing God's Peace to Disaster. An important online booklet produced by Church World Service (CWS) Emergency Response Program that addresses spiritual needs of disaster survivors. See http://www.cwserp.org/training/spcare/spcare.pdf.

The Disaster Chaplain: Bringing God's Presence to Trauma Victims. An online booklet produced by Church World Service (CWS) Emergency Response Program on what chaplains can do to address the spiritual and psychological needs of disaster victims. See http://www.cwserp.org/training/Chaplain.pdf.

Prepare to Care: Guide to Disaster Ministry in Your Congregation. This online pamphlet produced by CWS describes specific ways of working together before and after disasters to effectively respond to people in need. This is a very readable 50-page periodical. See http://www.cwserp.org/training/ptc/carecon.pdf.

"Emotional, Spiritual Needs Emerge Throughout Response to 'Operation Noble Eagle': Salvation Army Provides Guidance and Support for Displaced Survivors of Pentagon Attack." An article describing the response of the Salvation Army to the 9/11 Pentagon attack. See http://www.prnewswire.com/cgi-bin/stories. pl?ACCT=104&STORY=/www/story/09-20-2001/0001576055&EDATE

"Clergy and Psychiatrists: Opportunities for Expert Dialogue." This article, published in the March 2003 issue of *Psychiatric Times*, talks about the collaboration of clergy and mental health practitioners post-9/11. See http://www. psychiatrictimes.com/p030336.html.

"Religious Care in Coping with Terrorism." This is a book chapter written by Rabbi Zahara Davidowitz-Farkas, a certified chaplain and disaster specialist. For a copy, contact her at zdavidowitz@mindspring.com or davidowitzz@arcgny.org.

Handbook of Religion and Health (Oxford University Press, 2001). The thirty-five book chapters of this comprehensive review of history, research, and discussion of religion and health span mental and physical health, from positive emotions, anxiety, substance abuse, and depression to immune function, cancer, heart disease, stroke, chronic pain, disability, and other physical conditions. The appendix lists 1,200 separate scientific studies on religion and health that are reviewed and rated on 0–10 scale, followed by 2,000 references and an extensive index for rapid topic identification.

Handbook of Religion and Mental Health (Academic Press, 1998). This book describes how religious beliefs and practices from the major world religions relate to mental health and influence mental health care. Chapters describe research on the association between religion and personality, coping behavior, anxiety, depression, psychoses, and successes in psychotherapy, and discuss specific religions and their perspectives on mental health. However, this book is really for the clinician who needs information on how to treat people from different religious faiths.

Comprehensive Health Disaster Plan for a Faith Community

I have taken a key section of the DHHS publication Mental Health All-Hazards Disaster Planning Guidance (MHDPG) and edited it to apply to faith communities needing guidance on developing a detailed plan in responding to mental health needs of congregants and members of the broader community following disasters. The MHDPG was intended to "provide direction and support tailored specifically for State and local mental health leaders as they create and/or revise all-hazards response plans. In particular, the document provides counsel to

States on considerations for the planning process, and for actual plan content." In the back of this report is Appendix A, titled "Elements of an All-Hazards State Disaster Plan." I present this material *verbatim*, except for some minor editing and exclusion of material not relevant to faith communities. This is only a summary or outline, and readers should consult the original MHDPG document for details on each line item. A PDF file of the original MHDPG authored by Charles G. Curie (administrator at SAMHSA) and Robert W. Glover (executive director, National Association of State Mental Health Program Directors) is available on the SAMHSA Web site.[3]

Elements of an All-Hazards Faith-Community Disaster Mental Health Plan

1. Introductory Material
   A. Signature page
   B. Dated title page
   C. Record of changes
   D. Record of distribution
   E. Table of contents

2. Executive Summary
   Summary describing basic plan

3. Purpose
   General statement of plan's purpose

4. Situation and Assumptions–General
   A. Assumptions (limits of *faith community* activities, highest probability scenarios, etc.)
   B. Situation (probable impact, vulnerable/special populations, including low probability/high impact events, etc.)
   C. Include matrix of events if desired

5. Concept of Operations–General (sequence and scope of response)
   A. Overview of approach (what should happen, when, who directs?)
   B. Division of responsibility (*faith community*, Local, State, Federal, etc.)
   C. General sequence of actions before, during, after event
   D. Who is authorized to request aid, and in which situations?

6. Authorities and References
   Citation of legal authorities and reference documents as appropriate

7. Organization and Assignment of Responsibilities
   A. Listing, by position, of the types of tasks to be performed (matrix of primary/secondary/shared responsibilities)
   B. Documents tasks of *faith community*: definition of objective, charac-

terization of the situation, general plan of action, delegation of responsibilities, information on resources and administrative support necessary to accomplish tasks. Includes description of treatment responsibilities (internal/external)

C. Describes local, State, and Federal tasks outside *faith community* authority

D. Tasks related to other governmental levels and organizations (e.g., SMHA, county and city government, Red Cross, FEMA, SAMHSA/CMHS, Department of Justice, etc.)

E. Describes coordination with other *faith communities*, SMHA, other components of State and local government health department, substance abuse agency, criminal justice, law enforcement, fire and rescue, agriculture (including extension service and veterinary services), parks and recreation, animal care and control, victim services, social services, and education

F. Ensures connectivity to SMHA and SEMA and federal response plans

8. Administration, Logistics, Legal

   A. Administration–Recording and reporting program activities

   B. Administration–Recording and reporting expenditures and obligations

   C. Administration–Recording and reporting human resources utilization

   D. Administration–Management of volunteer offers/services

   E. Logistics–Arrangements for support needs (food, water, fuel, etc.)

   F. Logistics–Provision for self-support for at least 72 hours

   G. Logistics–Replacement/repair of damaged/destroyed essential equipment

   H. Logistics–Access of personnel to impacted area (criteria method, transportation)

   I. Logistics–Availability, transport, administration, safeguarding

   J. Logistics–Existence and scope of mutual aid agreements with other FBO and government organizations

   K. Legal–Issues including licensing, informed consent, confidentiality, providers licensed in other jurisdictions, personal, professional, and organization liability, or other procurement rules during emergencies

9. Plan Development and Maintenance

   Describes who is responsible for modifications and updating, ensuring coordination of faith community activity with State Mental Health Association and other State emergency planning elements

10. Communications
    A. Situation assumptions (types of situations likely to occur–should relate to earlier assumptions, types of communications necessary such as telephone, data, etc.)
    B. Methods of communication among *faith communities*, SMHA, local mental health agencies, State psychiatric hospitals, other psychiatric facilities, community-based treatment facilities, State emergency management, regional or field offices, emergency medical services, hospitals and clinics, shelter facilities. Ensure *faith communities* are on notification list from regional SEMA or SMHA (if not Governor's Office)
    C. Alternatives in the event of failed communication capacity
    D. Availability of technical expertise (within congregation)

11. Public Information
    A. Communications strategy
    B. Identification of responsibility
    C. Existence of public information material (fact sheets, guides, multiple languages, access to services, distribution of materials, etc.)
    D. Relationship with State emergency office public information officer
    E. Identified means of disseminating information

12. Warning: Mobilization Related to Internal Mental Health Systems
    A. Internal–Links with State emergency warning activities
    B. Internal–Describes methods and procedures for notifying staff and volunteers
    C. Internal–Establishes policies and procedures (e.g., sending staff home, holding staff in place, recall of essential staff, evacuation of facilities, etc.)
    D. External–Identifies groups with special warning needs (e.g., persons who are deaf)

13. Evacuation
    A. Plan for evacuation of *faith community* offices and facilities
    B. Plan for alternate sites ("hot," "warm," and "cold" sites as appropriate)
    C. Clear linkage with State emergency management evacuation plans and operations and SMHA or . . .
    D. Plan for services at shelters/mass care facilities (coordinated with SMHA or other local authorized group)

14. Mass Care
    A. Documentation of coordination of *faith community's* plan with State emergency management mass care plan/SMHA mass care plan
    B. Links with Red Cross special populations facilities and other National Voluntary Organizations Active in Disasters (NVOAD)

15. Health and Medical
    A. Documentation of coordination with State emergency management health and medical plan staffing, logistics, costs
    B. Provision of mental health services/consultation as part of State's emergency medical plan (Emergency Support Function #8, VA re sources, etc.) in coordination with SMHA plan (whenever possible)
    C. Roles identified in areas of services/consultation to primary victims, secondary victims, response and recovery workers, incident command, public information, body identification and recovery, mortuary services, other State agencies and departments (e.g., health epidemiology, education, social services, etc.)
    D. Documentation of coordination with Red Cross mental health services
    E. Documentation of coordination with Red Cross health services

16. Resource Management
    A. Purpose–Documents means, organization, and process by which *faith community* will find, obtain, allocate, and distribute necessary resources
    B. Personnel
    C. Transportation for staff
    D. Communications equipment
    E. Emergency equipment as necessary
    F. Mass care supplies
    G. Intrastate mutual aid
    H. Management of volunteers
    I. Availability of aid from other States, *faith communities,* and Federal government
    J. Plan for maintaining financial and legal accountability
    K. Resources for initial and ongoing needs assessment

17. All-Hazards Specific Planning Materials (Natural and Accidental)
    A. Plan allows for accommodation of unique aspects of hazards
    B. Identifies nature of hazard
    C. Identifies areas of high risk
    D. Flooding (flash and slow rising) and dam failure
    E. Hazardous materials (including chemicals)

    F. Hurricane/Tsunami

    G. Fire

    H. Earthquake

    I. Military chemical agents and munitions

    J. Radiological hazards (medical usage, educational institutions, military, manufacturing companies, transport of nuclear material)

    K. Nuclear power plant(s)

    L. Nuclear conflict (war)

    M. Snow/ice

    N. Tornado

    O. Civil unrest/community violence

    P. Other(s) (specify)

18. Terrorism

    A. Describes nature of potential hazards (chemical, biological, nuclear/radiological, explosive, cyber, combined)

    B. Potential nearby targets are identified (and/or reflective of State emergency plan)

    C. Describes environment, populations, urbanicity, infrastructure, transport patterns, airports, trains/subways, government facilities, recreation facilities, military installations, HazMat facilities, other high-risk targets such as financial institutions, universities, hospitals, research institutes, schools, daycare centers, and resources

    D. *Faith community* plan reflects knowledge of and integration with State emergency plan with respect to warning, communication, emergency public information, protective actions, mass care, health and medical annex, resource management

    E. Describes links to health and medical entities for purposes of assisting in screening potential victims for mental disorders and psychogenic symptomatology, functional impairment, substance abuse, etc.

    F. Describes links with State public health structure for surveillance, screening, consultation, intervention planning, risk communication

    G. Describes *faith community's* role in risk communication planning and response

    H. Describes *faith community's* participation in exercises and drills

19. Continuity of Operations

    A. Contains overview of goals of *faith community's* Continuity of Operations Plan (e.g., to maintain/reestablish vital functions during the first 72 hours following an event that would seriously compromise or halt normal operations)

  B. Identifies vital functions to be maintained within first 72 hours

  C. Identifies vital records/data necessary to function within first 72 hours

  D. Describes plans related to human resources (e.g., essential staff, staff notification, family support)

  E. Describes alternate locations of essential operations

  F. Describes transportation and staff support

  G. Describes alternate vital record/document sites (e.g., assurance of access to disaster plan, staff rosters)

20. Other Special Planning Concerns

  A. Documentation of regional or multi–*faith community* planning and coordination

  B. Describes various issues around licensing within State, scope of practice, etc.

  C. Documentation of plans to prepare and support *faith community* staff and volunteers during and following deployment under plan (physical, health, special medical needs, family support, psychological)

  D. Documentation of plans to prepare and support emergency service responders (e.g., police, fire, hospital emergency department staff, mortuary workers) during and following deployment

  E. Describes *faith community's* role in crisis and emergency risk communication

  F. Ensures *faith community's* role in disaster training and exercises

21. Standard Operating Procedures and Checklists

  A. Contains applicable standard operating procedures

  B. Contains applicable checklists (e.g., emergency contact numbers, lists of facilities, etc.)

Research on Faith and the Faith Communities During Disasters

Below are listed individual research studies that explore the role of religion in coping with disasters and the role of the faith community in responding to disasters. These are listed by type of disaster in alphabetical order.

Airline Crash

Black, J. W. 1987. The libidinal cocoon: A nurturing retreat for the families of plane crash victims. *Hospital and Community Psychiatry* 38 (12): 1322–26.

Chemical Spill

Chaffee, M., C. Conway-Welch, and V. Stephens. 2001. Bioterrorism in the United States: Take it seriously. *AJN, American Journal of Nursing* 101 (11): 59, 61.

Earthquake

Priya, K. R. 2002. Suffering and healing among the survivors of Bhuj earthquake. *Psychological Studies* 47 (1–3): 106–12.

Fires

Lindy, J. D., M. C. Grace, and B. L. Green. 1981. Survivors: Outreach to a reluctant population. *American Journal of Orthopsychiatry* 51:468–78.

Green, B. L., M. C. Grace, and G. C. Gleser. 1985. Identifying survivors at risk: Long-term impairment following the Beverly Hills Supper Club fire. *Journal of Consulting and Clinical Psychology* 53:672–78.

Floods

Echterling, L. G., C. Bradfield, and M. L. Wylie. 1988. Responses of urban and rural ministers to a natural disaster. *Journal of Rural Community Psychology* 9 (1): 36–46.

Powell, B. J., and E. C. Penick. 1983. Psychological distress following a natural disaster: A one-year follow-up of 98 flood victims. *Journal of Community Psychology* 11 (3): 269–76.

Smith, B. W., K. I. Pargament, C. Brant, and J. M. Oliver. 2000. Noah revisited: Religious coping by church members and the impact of the 1993 Midwest flood. *Journal of Community Psychology* 28 (2): 169–86.

Hurricanes

Aderibigbe, Y. A., R. M. Bloch, and A. Pandurangi. 2003. Emotional and somatic distress in eastern North Carolina: Help-seeking behaviors. *International Journal of Social Psychiatry* 49 (2): 126–41.

Gillard, M., and D. Paton. 1999. Disaster stress following a hurricane: The role of religious differences in the Fijian Islands. *Australasian Journal of Disaster and Trauma Studies* 3 (2): n.p.

Haines, V. A., J. S. Hurlbert, and J. J. Beggs. 1996. Exploring the determinants of support provision: Provider characteristics, personal networks, community contexts, and support following life events. *Journal of Health and Social Behavior* 37 (3): 252–64.

Sattler, D. N., B. A. Hamby, J. M. Winkler, and C. Kaiser. 1994. Hurricane Iniki: Psychological functioning following disaster. Presented at the annual meeting of the American Psychological Association, Los Angeles, Ca.

Weinrich, S., S. B. Hardin, and M. Johnson. 1990. Nurses respond to Hurricane Hugo victims' disaster stress. *Archives of Psychiatric Nursing* 4:195–205.

Mining Disaster

Kroll-Smith, J., and S. R. Couch. 1987. A chronic technical disaster and the irrelevance of religious meaning: The case of Centralia, Pennsylvania. *Journal for the Scientific Study of Religion* 26 (1): 25–37.

Nuclear

Frank, J. D. 1984. Nuclear death: An unprecedented challenge to psychiatry and religion. *American Journal of Psychiatry* 141 (11): 1343–48 (opinion piece; no research).

Technological Crisis

Powell, L., M. Hickson III, W. R. Self, and J. Bodon. 2001. The role of religion and responses to the Y2K macro-crisis. *North American Journal of Psychology* 3 (2): 295–302.

Terrorist Acts

Everly, G. S. 2003. Pastoral crisis intervention in response to terrorism. *International Journal of Emergency Mental Health* 5 (1): 1–2.

Nixon, S. J., J. Schorr, A. Boudreaux, and R. D. Vincent. 1999. Perceived sources of support and their effectiveness for Oklahoma City firefighters. *Psychiatric Annals* (2): 101–5.

Pargament, K. I., B. W. Smith, H. G. Koenig, and L. Perez. 1998. Patterns of positive and negative religious coping with major life stressors. *Journal for the Scientific Study of Religion* 37:710–24 (Oklahoma City bombing).

Peterson, C., and M. E. Seligman. 2003. Character strengths before and after September 11. *Psychological Science* 14 (4): 381–84.

Schuster, M. A., B. D. Stein, L. H. Jaycox, R. L. Collins, G. N. Marshall, M. N. Elliott, A. J. Zhou, D. E. Kanouse, J. L. Morrison, and S. H. Berry. 2001. A national survey of stress reactions after the September 11, 2001, terrorist attacks. *New England Journal of Medicine* 345:1507–12.

Tornados and Cyclones

Chinnici, R. 1985. Pastoral care following a natural disaster. *Pastoral Psychology* 33 (4): 245–54.

Nelson, L., and R. R. Dynes. 1976. The impact of devotionalism and attendance on ordinary and emergency helping behavior. *Journal for the Scientific Study of Religion.* 15 (1): 47–59.

North, C. S., E. M. Smith, R. E. McCool, and P. E. Lightcap. 1989. Acute postdisaster coping and adjustment. *Journal of Traumatic Stress* 2 (3): 353–60.

Taylor, A. J. W. 1998. Observations from a cyclone stress/trauma assignment in the Cook Islands. *Traumatology* 4 (1): article 3. See http://www.fsu.edu/~trauma/art3v4i1.html (retrieved November 20, 2003).

War Trauma

Kaplan, Z., M. A. Matar, R. Kamin, T. Sadan, and H. Cohen. 2005. Stress-related responses after 3 years of exposure to terror in Israel: Are ideological-religious factors associated with resilience? *Journal of Clinical Psychiatry* 66:1146–54.

Pargament, K. I., K. Ishler, E. Dubow, P. Stanik, R. Rouiller, P. Crowe, E. Cullman, M. Albert, and B. J. Royster. 1994. Methods of religious coping with the Gulf War: Cross-sectional and longitudinal analyses. *Journal for the Scientific Study of Religion* 33:347–61.

Zimmerman, G., and W. Weber. 2000. Care for the caregivers: A program for Canadian military chaplains after serving in NATO and United Nations peacekeeping missions in the 1990s. *Military Medicine* 165 (9): 687–90.

Miscellaneous

Everly, G. S. 2000. The role of pastoral crisis intervention in disasters, terrorism, violence, and other community crises. *International Journal of Emergency Mental Health* 2 (3): 139–42.

Nelson, L., and R. R. Dynes. 1976. The impact of devotionalism and attendance on ordinary and emergency helping behavior. *Journal for the Scientific Study of Religion* 15 (1): 47–59.

North, C. S., and B. A. Hong. 2000. Project CREST: A new model for mental health intervention after a community disaster. *American Journal of Public Health* 90 (7): 1057–58.

Glossary of Terms and Definitions

A number of terms are used in this book that may be unfamiliar to the reader. Therefore, I am providing definitions of some of these terms by alphabetical order.[1] They will be important in communicating with groups during disaster preparation and disaster response. Understanding this disaster language will also enable the reader to more quickly assimilate the material presented in this book.

Acute Stress Disorder (ASD): If the full symptom criteria for PTSD (see below) are present for less than one month, then it is called an acute stress disorder.

Center for Mental Health Services (CMHS): This is a department within the Substance Abuse and Mental Health Services Administration, within the U.S. Department of Health and Human Services.

Crisis Counseling Program: A federally funded counseling program that may be useful for low-income disaster victims who need help beyond what the faith community can offer.

Critical Incident Stress Debriefing: This involves the counseling given to a disaster victim immediately following a highly stressful disaster or traumatic event (war).

Department of Health and Human Services (DHHS): DHHS is an agency of the U.S. government charged with protecting the health of all Americans and providing essential human services, especially for those who are least able to help themselves. It gives out over 60,000 grants each year to ensure that this happens.

Disaster: This is usually a physically traumatic event that causes major loss of life (10 persons or more), serious injuries of many more, and/or extensive property damage. Such events may involve storms such as hurricanes or tornadoes, earthquakes, volcanoes, fires, unintended chemical or nuclear spills, or acts of terrorism including biological (anthrax), chemical, nuclear, other explosives (Oklahoma City), or aviation-related incidents (September 11).

Disaster Assistance Program: A program designed to prepare for, plan, and respond to the mental health needs of disaster victims and emergency responders of local, state, and federally declared disasters.

Disaster District Chairman: Usually a police officer (trooper at the level of lieutenant) responsible for incident command who coordinates response between the State Operations Center and local emergency services.

Disaster Field Office: This is the state or federal disaster operation's headquarters that is set up near a disaster.

Division of Emergency Management (DEM): Each state has such a division in the government directed by the governor that handles all of the emergencies and disasters that occur within that state.

Emergency Management Coordinator: The person in charge at the city and/or county level whose job is to coordinate and integrate local resources during a disaster.

Emergency Management Services (EMS): Usually refers to first responders in emergencies, such as police, firefighters, or emergency medical services.

Federal Coordinating Officer: The FEMA employee in charge of the disaster field office and the disaster or event.

Generalized Anxiety Disorder: A condition characterized by at least six months of chronic worry about many different, seemingly unrelated concerns, which makes life difficult and interferes with social or occupational functioning. Worry or anxiety symptoms may include restlessness or feeling keyed up, easy fatigue, difficulty concentrating, irritability, muscle tension, or sleep disturbance.

Grief: A painful emotional experience that accompanies the loss of a loved one or of material possessions (or job) to which one is attached. This may also apply to loss of health or loss of the ability to function.

Hyperarousal: A state of increased mental, emotional, and physiological alertness that occurs during periods of crisis, threat, or disaster.

Immediate Services Program: A sixty-day crisis-counseling program funded by FEMA/SAMHSA.

Incident Command System: The national model for managing and coordinating emergency operations in response to disasters.

Major Depression (clinical depression): Seriously depressed mood or loss of interest lasting for at least two weeks that interferes with social or occupational functioning and is accompanied by at least four of the following eight symptoms: weight loss or gain, insomnia or excessive sleeping, difficulty concentrating, feeling worthless or guilty, loss of energy, moving more slowly or excessively restless, loss of social or sexual interest, and suicidal thoughts.

Mitigation: Mitigation involves attempts to minimize the impact of natural disasters by educating the public and developing regulations to make homes, businesses, and communities as safe as possible from damage induced by hurricanes, floods, tornadoes, earthquakes, or other types of natural or technological disasters or terrorist attacks.

National Association of State Mental Health Program Directors: This organization consists of the directors of all state mental health associations (SMHA). Its Web site can help FBOs locate the nearest SMHA office in their area.

Panic or Panic Attack: A feeling of severe anxiety and fear that usually lasts for only a few minutes and is accompanied by shortness of breath, rapid heart rate, and a sense of impending doom or loss of control.

Panic Disorder: A condition characterized by recurrent and unexpected panic attacks (at least four within a single month) that may cause a person to alter his or her lifestyle to avoid situations likely to bring on an attack. At least one of the attacks must be followed by one month or longer of persistent concern about having additional attacks, worry about the implications of the attack, or a significant change in behavior. Panic attacks must be severe enough to interfere with the person's ability to function.

Post-Traumatic Stress Disorder (PTSD): According to the Diagnostic and Statistical Manual, 4th Edition (DSM-IV), post-traumatic stress is considered a normal reaction to an abnormally stressful situation that elicits intense fear or helplessness and involves an actual or threatened death, serious injury, or a severe threat to oneself or others. Symptoms of PTSD include recurrent and intrusive distressing recollections or dreams of the event, avoidance of situations that remind the person of the trauma, emotional numbing, hypervigilance, and irritability. PTSD is diagnosed when symptoms are present for more than one month and functioning is impaired.

Rapid Assessment Unit: A unit within a state's Division of Emergency Management (DEM) that does initial damage assessments following a disaster.

Regular Services Program: A nine-month crisis counseling program that is federally funded through the Center for Mental Health Studies (CMHS) or Substance Abuse and Mental Health Services Administration (SAMHSA).

Risk Management: This is a program in some states designed to protect employees, the general public, and the agency's physical and financial assets by reducing and controlling risk from individual lawsuits.

State Coordinator: A DEM employee who is the federal counterpart at the disaster field office and in charge of the State's response to disaster.

State Crisis Consortium: Involves a collaborative effort between several State agencies in order to plan for and respond to disasters and emergencies.

State Emergency Management Council: This counsel consists of thirty-three agencies within a state that are prepared to respond to disaster or other emergencies throughout the state.

State Emergency Response Team: This team is made up of state agency representatives that are responsible for rapid mobilization to respond immediately to disasters within a state.

Substance Abuse and Mental Health Services Administration (SAMHSA): An agency of the Department of Health and Human Services, SAMHSA works closely with FEMA in providing mental health information to victims of disasters and offering grants for counseling outreach and for the training of crisis counselors to provide assistance after FEMA relief workers leave the area.

Traumatic Event: Any event that occurs outside the normal range of normal experience that is prone to cause intense fear, shock, helplessness, or a sense of overwhelming vulnerability or horror. I would include here a sense of spiritual disorientation or loss of faith.

Notes

Preface

1. Johanna Olson of Lutheran Disaster Relief staff, discussion with author, 2003; see http://www.elca.org/dcs/staff/olson.johanna.html.

Acknowledgments

1. Francis Gunn is a Catholic priest and trained mental health professional who was instrumental in the clergy response to the World Trade Center terrorist attacks in New York City on September 11, working closely with NYFD personnel. He is often sought as a consultant on spiritual issues (Spiritfx@aol.com).

2. Zahara Davidowitz-Farkas is a rabbi and certified chaplain. She is executive director of the Institute for Disaster Spiritual Care in New York City and the author of "Religious Care in Coping with Terrorism" (zdavidowitz@mindspring.com or davidow-itzz@arcgny.org).

3. Johanna Olson is on the staff of Lutheran Disaster Response and is a consultant for the National Organization of Volunteers Active during Disasters (NOVAD) in the area of spiritual care following disasters (JOlson@elca.org).

4. David Pollock is executive director of the Jewish Community Relations Council of New York. He has produced some excellent training material for faith-based organizations, including the booklet *Emergency Planning: Creating Disaster and Crisis Response Systems for Jewish Organizations* (pollockd@jcrcny.org).

Introduction

1. S. D. Soloman, "Research Issues in Assessing Disaster's Effects," in *Psychosocial Aspects of Disaster*, ed. R. Gist and B. Lubin (New York: Wiley, 1989), 308–40.

2. C. Long, "Disaster Losses on the Rise," *Disaster Relief*, May 21, 1999; see http://www.disasterrelief.org/Disasters/990521costs/.

3. "Senators: Cut Fat to Fund Katrina Recovery," *CNN.com*, Washington, D.C., September 19, 2005.

4. "Katrina's Official Deaths Top 1,000," *CNN.com*, New Orleans, La., September 21, 2005.

5. See Web site: http://en.wikipedia.org/wiki/2004_Indian_Ocean_earthquake (last accessed 10/21/05).

6. See Web site: http://www.npr.org/templates/story/story.php?storyId=4954200&sourceCode=gaw (last accessed 11/14/05).

7. Ahmad M., "UN: Quake Victims Need More Global Help," *Associated Press*, October 21, 2005.

8. http://news.nationalgeographic.com/news/2005/10/photogalleries/ earthquake/ (last accessed 11/14/05).

9. M. A. Schuster, B. D. Stein, L. H. Jaycox, R. L. Collins, G. N. Marshall, M. N. Elliott, A. J. Zhou, D. E. Kanouse, J. L. Morrison, and S. H. Berry, "A National Survey of Stress Reactions after the September 11, 2001, Terrorist Attacks," *New England Journal of Medicine* 345 (2001): 1507–12.

10. American Red Cross, *The Lifecycle of a Disaster: Ritual and Practice: Understanding the Impact of the 9/11 Terrorist Attacks on Faith Communities and Their Leaders* (New York: American Red Cross, 2002).

11. Jeff Seidel, "Katrina's Aftermath: Churches Take Charge and Care for Survivors," *Detroit Free Press*, September 5, 2005 (the story appeared on Monday, one week after the hurricane hit).

Chapter 1

1. Kazumi Adachi, Sandra Bertman, Charles Corr, Jerre Cory, Kenneth Doka, Kathleen Gilbert, Esther Gjertsen, Geoffrey Glassock, Christopher Hall, Robert Hansson, Isa Jaramillo, Kjell Kallenberg, Marcia Lattanzi-Licht, Norelle Lickiss, Peggy Oechsle, Kevin Ann Oltjenbruns, Danai Papadatou, Colin Murray Parkes, Donna Schuurman, and William Worden, "Assumptions and Principles about Psychosocial Aspects of Disasters," *Death Studies* 26, no. 6 (2002): 449–62.

2. Ronald W. Perry and Michael K. Lindell, "Understanding Citizen Response to Disasters with Implications for Terrorism," *Journal of Contingencies and Crisis Management* 11, no. 2 (2003): 49–60.

3. Adachi et al., "Assumptions and Principles about Psychosocial Aspects of Disasters," 455.

4. Mitchell G. Weiss, Benedetto Saraceno, Shekhar Saxena, and Mark van Ommeren, "Mental Health in the Aftermath of Disasters: Consensus and Controversy," *Journal of Nervous and Mental Disease* 191, no. 9 (2003): 611–15.

5. "Despair among Some Katrina Survivors: Some Say It's More Difficult Now than Immediately after Storm," *Associated Press*, September 23, 2005; posted on *CNN. com,* September 24, 2005.

6. J. Frieden, "Katrina Survivors' Psychiatric Needs Unpredictable: 'Cascade of Disasters' Magnifies Trauma," *Clinical Psychiatry News* 33, no. 10 (2005): 1, 7.

7. Anthony V Rubonis and Leonard Bickman, "Psychological Impairment in the Wake of Disaster: The Disaster-psychopathology Relationship," *Psychological Bulletin* 109, no. 3 (1991): 384–99.

8. R. C. Kessler, A. Sonnega, E. Bromet, M. Hughes et al., "Posttraumatic Stress Disorder in the National Comorbidity Survey," *Archives of General Psychiatry* 52, no. 12 (1995): 1048–60.

9. S. Zisook, Y. Chentsova-Dutton, and S. R. Shuchter, "PTSD Following Bereavement," *Annals of Clinical Psychiatry* 10, no. 4 (1998): 157–63.

10. N. C. Andreason, "Post-traumatic Stress Disorder," in *The Comprehensive Textbook of Psychiatry*, ed. H. I. Kaplan and B. J. Sadock (Baltimore, Md.: Williams & Wilkins, 1985), 918–24.

11. Zisook et al., "PTSD Following Bereavement."

12. Daniella David, Thomas A. Mellman, Lourdes M. Mendoza, Renee Kulick-Bell et al., "Psychiatric Morbidity Following Hurricane Andrew," *Journal of Traumatic Stress* 9, no. 3 (1996): 607–12.

13. Bonnie L. Green, Jacob D. Lindy, Mary C. Grace, Goldine C. Gleser et al., "Buffalo Creek Survivors in the Second Decade: Stability of Stress Symptoms," *American Journal of Orthopsychiatry* 60, no. 1 (1990): 43–54.

14. B. L. Green, J. D. Lindy, M. C. Grace, and A. C. Leonard, "Chronic Posttraumatic Stress Disorder and Diagnostic Comorbidity in a Disaster Sample," *Journal of Nervous and Mental Disease* 180, no. 12 (1992): 760–66.

15. B. C. Chamberlin, "Mayo Seminars in Psychiatry: The Psychological Aftermath of Disaster," *Journal of Clinical Psychiatry* 41, no. 7 (1980): 238–44.

16. Carol S. North, Sara Jo Nixon, Sheryll Shariat, Sue Mallonee, J. Curtis McMillen, Edward L. Spitznagel, and Elizabeth M. Smith, "Psychiatric Disorders among Survivors of the Oklahoma City Bombing," *Journal of the American Medical Association* 282, no. 8 (1999): 755–62.

17. Sandro Galea, Jennifer Ahern, Heidi Resnick, Dean Kilpatrick, Michael Bucuvalas, Joel Gold, and David Vlahov, "Psychological Sequelae of the September 11 Terrorist Attacks in New York City," *New England Journal of Medicine* 346, no. 13 (2002): 982–87.

18. Z. Kaplan, M. A. Matar, R. Kamin, T. Sadan, and H. Cohen, "Stress-related Responses after 3 Years of Exposure to Terror in Israel: Are Ideological-religious Factors Associated with Resilience?" *Journal of Clinical Psychiatry* 66 (2005): 1146–54.

19. R. A. Kulka, J. A. Fairbank, K. B. Jordan, D. Weiss, and A. Cranston, *Trauma and the Vietnam War Generations: Report of the Findings from the National Vietnam Veterans Readjustment Study* (New York: Brunner/Mazel, 1990).

20. C. W. Hoge, C. A. Castro, S. C. Messer, D. McGurk, D. I. Cotting, and R. L. Koffman, "Combat Duty in Iraq and Afghanistan, Mental Health Problems, and Barriers to Care," *New England Journal of Medicine* 351, no. 1 (2004): 13–22.

21. Fran H. Norris, Krzysztof Kaniasty, M. Lori Conrad, Gregory L. Inman, and Arthur D. Murphy, "Placing Age Differences in Cultural Context: A Comparison of the Effects of Age on PTSD after Disasters in the United States, Mexico, and Poland," *Journal of Clinical Geropsychology* 8, no. 3 (2002): 153–73.

22. Mitsuko P. Shannon, Christopher J. Lonigan, A. J. Finch, and Charlotte M. Taylor, "Children Exposed to Disaster: I. Epidemiology of Post-traumatic Symptoms and Symptom Profiles," *Journal of the American Academy of Child and Adolescent Psychiatry* 33, no. 1 (1994): 80–93.

23. A. C. McFarlane, "The Longitudinal Course of Posttraumatic Morbidity," *Journal of Nervous and Mental Disease* 176 (1988): 30–39.

24. A. C. McFarlane, "The Phenomenology of Posttraumatic Stress Disorders Following a Natural Disaster," *Journal of Nervous and Mental Disease* 176, no. 1 (1988): 22–29.

25. D. W. Foy, *Treating Post-Traumatic Stress Disorder: Cognitive-behavioral Strategies* (New York: Guilford Press, 1992).

26. Galea et al., "Psychological Sequelae of the September 11 Terrorist Attacks in New York City."

27. M. S. Gibbs, "Factors in the Victim That Mediate between Disaster and Psychopathology: A Review," *Journal of Traumatic Stress* 2, no. 4 (1989): 489–514.

28. N. Breslau, G. C. Davis, P. Andreski, and E. Peterson, "Traumatic Events and Posttraumatic Stress Disorder in an Urban Population of Young Adults," *Archives of General Psychiatry* 48 (1991): 216–22.

29. Gibbs, "Factors in the Victim That Mediate between Disaster and Psychopathology: A Review."

30. Ibid.

31. C. R. Brewin, B. Andrews, and J. D. Valentine, "Meta-analysis of Risk Factors for PTSD in Exposed Adults," *Journal of Consulting and Clinical Psychology* 68 (2000): 748–66.

32. Francis Gunn provided this original information specifically for this book in 2003.

33. J. P. Wilson and T. A. Moran, "Psychological Trauma: Posttraumatic Stress Disorder and Spirituality," *Journal of Psychology and Theology* 26, no. 2 (1998): 168–78.

34. R. Janoff-Bulman, "The Aftermath of Victimization: Rebuilding Shattered Assumptions," in *Trauma and Its Wake*, vol. 1: *The Study and Treatment of Post-Traumatic Stress Disorder*, ed. C. R. Figley (New York: Brunner/Mazel, 1985), 15–35.

35. E. Erikson, *Childhood and Society* (New York: W. W. Norton, 1963).

36. J. L. Herman, *Trauma and Its Recovery* (New York: Basic Books, 1992), 52, quoted in Wilson and Moran, "Psychological Trauma."

37. Wilson and Moran, "Psychological Trauma," 172.

38. Matthew 27:46, *New International Version of the Holy Bible* (New Brunswick, N.J.: International Bible Society, 1978, 1983).

39. K. I. Pargament, H. G. Koenig, N. Tarakeshwar, and J. Hahn, "Religious Struggle as a Predictor of Mortality among Medically Ill Elderly Patients: A Two-year Longitudinal Study," *Archives of Internal Medicine* 161 (2001): 1881–85.

40. J. Brende and E. McDonald, "Post-traumatic Spiritual Alienation and Recovery in Vietnam Combat Veterans," *Spirituality Today* 41 (1989): 319–40.

41. F. M. Ochberg, "Posttraumatic Therapy," in *International Handbook of Traumatic Stress Syndromes*, ed. J. Wilson and B. Raphael (New York: Plenum Press, 1993), 773–83.

42. B. H. Chang, K. M. Skinner, and U. Boehmer, "Religion and Mental Health among Women Veterans with Sexual Assault Experience," *International Journal of Psychiatry in Medicine* 31 (2001): 77–96.

43. B. H. Chang, K. M. Skinner, C. Zhou, and L. E. Kazis, "The Relationship between Sexual Assault, Religiosity and Mental Health among Male Veterans," *International Journal of Psychiatry in Medicine* 33, no. 3 (2003): 223–40.

44. A. Fontana and R. Rosenheck, "Trauma, Change in Strength of Religious Faith, and Mental Health Service Use among Veterans Treated for PTSD," *Journal of Nervous and Mental Disease* 192 (2004): 579–84.

45. C. L. Park, L. H. Cohen, and R. L. Murch, "Assessment and Prediction of Stress-related Growth," *Journal of Personality* 64 (1996): 71–105.

46. Ibid.

47. H. G. Koenig, K. I. Pargament, and J. Nielsen, "Religious Coping and Health Status in Medically Ill Hospitalized Older Adults," *Journal of Nervous and Mental Disease* 186, no. 9 (1998): 513–21.

Chapter 2

1. Adapted from FEMA Web site, http://www.fema.gov/about/history.shtm.

2. See http://clinton.senate.gov/news/statements/details.cfm?id=245265.

3. See http://federaltimes.com/index2.php?S=1097273.

4. See http://training.fema.gov/emiweb/IS/.

5. Adapted from American Red Cross Web site, http://www.redcross.org/faq/0,1096,0_315_,00.html

6. See http://www.redcross.org/donate/goods/.

7. See http://www.nvoad.org/history1.php#principles.

8. See http://www.nvoad.org/membersdb.php?members=National.

9. See http://www.nvoad.org/history4.php.

10. See http://www.trynova.org/AB/aboutnova.html.

11. See http://www.disasternews.net/index3.php.

12. See http://www.disasterrelief.org/.

13. See http://www.icisf.org/.

14. See http://www.fema.gov/rrr/gaheop.shtm.

15. See http://www.dem.dcc.state.nc.us/Em1.htm.

16. Ibid.

17. See http://www.nasmhpd.org/members.htm#A.

18. See http://www.mentalhealth.org/publications/allpubs/SMA03-3829/default.asp.

Chapter 3

1. The Gallup Organization, "Poll Topics and Trends," http://www.gallup.com/poll/topics/religion.asp (accessed January 5, 2004).

2. T. A. Cronan, R. M. Kaplan, L. Posner, E. Lumberg, and F. Kozin, "Prevalence of the Use of Unconventional Remedies for Arthritis in a Metropolitan Community," *Arthritis and Rheumatism* 32 (1989): 1604–7.

3. C. D. Samuel-Hodge, S. W. Headen, A. H. Skelly, A. F. Ingram, T. C. Keyserling, E. J. Jackson, A. S. Ammerman, and T. A. Elasy, "Influences on Day-to-day Self-management of Type 2 Diabetes among African-American Women," *Diabetes Care* 23 (2000): 928–33.

4. A. P. Tix and P. A. Frazier, "The Use of Religious Coping during Stressful Life Events," *Journal of Consulting and Clinical Psychology* 66 (1997): 411–22.

5. M. E. O'Brien, "Religious Faith and Adjustment to Long-term Hemodialysis," *Journal of Religion and Health* 21 (1982): 68–80.

6. R. A. Schnoll, L. L. Harlow, and L. Brower, "Spirituality, Demographic and Disease Factors, and Adjustment to Cancer," *Cancer Practice* 8 (2000): 298–304.

7. M.T. Halstead and J. I. Fernsler, "Coping Strategies of Long-term Cancer Survivors," *Cancer Nursing* 17, no. 2 (1994): 94–100.

8. A. L. Ai, R. E. Dunkle, C. Peterson, and S. F. Bolling, "The Role of Private Prayer in Psychological Recovery among Midlife and Aged Patients Following Cardiac Surgery (CABG)," *Gerontologist* 38 (1998): 591–601.

9. T. L. Saudia, M. R. Kinney, K. C. Brown, and L. Young-Ward, "Health Locus of Control and Helpfulness of Prayer," *Heart & Lung* 20 (1991): 60–65.

10. R. C. Harris, M. A. Dew, A. Lee, M. Amaya, L. Buches, D. Reetz, and G. Coleman, "The Role of Religion in Heart Transplant Recipients' Health and Well-Being," *Journal of Religion and Health* 34, no. 1 (1995): 17–32.

11. B. J. Matthees, Puree Anantachoti, M. J. Kreitzer, K. Savik, M. I. Hertz, and C. R. Gross, "Use of Complementary Therapies, Adherence, and Quality of Life in Lung Transplant Recipients," *Heart & Lung* 30 (2001): 258–68.

12. S. K. Avants, L. A. Warburton, and A. Margolin, "Spiritual and Religious Support in Recovery from Addiction among HIV-positive Injection Drug Users," *Journal of Psychoactive Drugs* 33 (2001): 39–45.

13. G. Ironson, G. F. Solomon, E. G. Balbin, C. O. Cleirigh, A. George, M. Kumar, D. Larson, and T. E. Woods, "Spirituality and Religiousness Are Associated with Long Survival, Health Behaviors, Less Distress, and Lower Cortisol in People Living with HIV/AIDS: The IWORSHIP Scale, Its Validity and Reliability," *Annals of Behavioral Medicine* 24 (2002): 34–48.

14. R. C. Stern, E. R. Canda, and C. F. Doershuk, "Use of Non-medical Treatment by Cystic Fibrosis Patients," *Journal of Adolescent Health* 13 (1992): 612–15.

15. M. Cooper-Effa, W. Blount, N. Kaslow, R. Rothenberg, and J. Eckman, "Role of Spirituality in Patients with Sickle Cell Disease," *Journal of the American Board of Family Practice* 14 (2001): 116–22.

16. P. L. Murphy, S. M. Albert, C. M. Weber, M. L. Del Bene, L. P. Rowland, "Impact of Spirituality and Religiousness on Outcomes in Patients with ALS," *Neurology* 55 (2000): 1581–84.

17. F. J. Keefe, G. Affleck, J. Lefebvre, L. Underwood, D. S. Caldwell, J. Drew, J. Egert, J. Gibson, and K. Pargament, "Giving with Rheumatoid Arthritis: The Role of Daily Spirituality and Daily Religious and Spiritual Coping," *Journal of Pain* 2, no. 2 (2001): 101–10.

18. T. J. Silber and M. Reilly, "Spiritual and Religious Concerns of the Hospitalized Adolescent," *Adolescence* 20, no. 77 (1985): 217–24.

19. H. G. Koenig, H. J. Cohen, D. G. Blazer, C. Pieper, K. G. Meador, F. Shelp, et al., "Religious Coping and Depression among Elderly, Hospitalized Medically Ill Men," *American Journal of Psychiatry* 149, no. 12 (1992): 1693–1700.

20. A. W. Braam, A. T. F. Beekman, D. J. H. Deeg, J. H. Smith, and W. van Tilburg, "Religiosity as a Protective or Prognostic Factor of Depression in Later Life: Results from the Community Survey in The Netherlands," *Acta Psychiatrica Scandinavia* 96 (1997): 199–205.

21. H. G. Koenig, L. K. George, and B. L. Peterson, "Religiosity and Remission of Depression in Medically Ill Older Patients," *American Journal of Psychiatry* 155, no. 4 (1998): 536–42.

22. K. I. Manton, "The Stress-buffering Role of Spiritual Support: Cross-sectional and Prospective Investigations," *Journal for the Scientific Study of Religion* 28 (1989): 310–23.

23. H. G. Koenig, L. K. George, and I. C. Siegler, "The Use of Religion and Other Emotion-regulating Coping Strategies among Older Adults," *Gerontologist* 28, no. 3 (1988): 303–10.

24. J. A. Mattlin, E. Wethington, and R. C. Kessler, "Situational Determinants of Coping and Coping Effectiveness," *Journal of Health and Social Behavior* 31 (1990): 103–22.

25. Kiri Walsh, Michael King; Louise Jones, Adrian Tookman, Robert Blizard, "Spiritual Beliefs May Affect Outcome of Bereavement: Prospective Study," *British Medical Journal* 324, no. 7353 (2002): 1551.

26. J. Ramirez-Johnson, C. Fayard, C. Garberoglio, and C. M. Ramirez, "Is Faith an Emotion? Faith as a Meaning-making Affective Process: An Example from Breast Cancer Patients," *American Behavioral Scientist* 45, no. 12 (2002): 1839–53.

27. K. I. Pargament, H. G. Koenig, N. Tarakeshwar, J. Hahn, "Religious Coping Methods as Predictors of Psychological, Physical, and Spiritual Outcomes among Medically Ill Elderly Patients: A Two-year Longitudinal Study," *Journal of Health Psychology* 9, no. 6 (2004): 713–30.

28. G. Fitchett, B. D. Rybarczyk, G. A. DeMarco, and J. J. Nicholas, "The Role of Religion in Medical Rehabilitation Outcomes: A Longitudinal Study," *Rehabilitation Psychology* 44, no. 4 (1999): 333–53.

29. Swasti Shrimali, and K. D. Broota, "Effect of Surgical Stress on Belief in God and Superstition: An in Situ Investigation," *Journal of Personality and Clinical Studies* 3, no. 2 (1987): 135–38.

30. K. I. Pargament, *The Psychology of Religion and Coping: Theory, Research, Practice* (New York: Guilford Press, 1997).

31. The Gallup Organization, "Poll Topics and Trends," http://www.gallup.com/poll/topics/religion.asp (accessed July 18, 2003).

32. C. G. Ellison and R. J. Taylor, "Turning to Prayer: Social and Situational Antecedents of Religious Coping among African Americans," *Review of Religious Research* 38 (1996): 111–31.

33. T. Pettersson, "Religion and Criminality: Structural Relationships between Church Involvement and Crime Rates in Contemporary Sweden," *Journal for the Scientific Study of Religion* 30 (1991): 279–91.

34. See World Values Survey, http://www.umich.edu/~newsinfo/Releases/1997/Dec97/r121097a.html.

35. M. Cederblad, L. Dahlin, and O. Hagnell, "Coping with Life Span Crises in a Group at Risk of Mental and Behavioral Disorders: From the Lundby Study," *Acta Psychiatrica Scandinavia* 91 (1995): 322–30.

36. P. Dekker and P. Ester, "Depillarization, Deconfessionalization, and

De-ideologization: Empirical Trends in Dutch Society 1958–1992," *Review of Religious Research* 37 (1996): 325–41.

37. Braam et al., "Religiosity as a Protective or Prognostic Factor of Depression in Later Life."

38. G. Ringdal, K. Gotestam, S. Kaasa, S. Kvinnslaud, and K. Ringdal, "Prognostic Factors and Survival in a Heterogeneous Sample of Cancer Patients," *British Journal of Cancer* 73 (1995): 1594–99.

39. A. Kesselring, M. J. Dodd, A. M. Lindsey, and A. L. Strauss, "Attitudes of Patients Living in Switzerland about Cancer and Its Treatment," *Cancer Nursing* 9 (1986): 77–85.

40. D. G. Ollendick and M. Hoffman, "Assessment of Psychological Reactions in Disaster Victims," *Journal of Community Psychology* 10 (1982): 157–67.

41. U. Patrick and W. K. Patrick, "Cyclone '78 in Sri Lanka—The Mental Health Trail," *British Journal of Psychiatry* 138 (1981): 210–16.

42. R. Lachman, "Behavior and Beliefs during the Recent Volcanic Eruption at Kapoho, Hawaii," *Science* 13 (1960): 1095–96.

43. J. G. Ahler and J. B. Tamney, "Some Functions of Religious Ritual in a Catastrophe," *Sociological Analysis* 25 (1964): 212–30.

44. J. H. Bushnell, "Hupa Reaction to the Trinity River Floods: Post-hoc Recourse to Aboriginal Belief," *Anthropological Quarterly* 42 (1969): 316–24.

45. A. J. W. Taylor, "Observations from a Cyclone Stress/Trauma Assignment in the Cook Islands," *Traumatology* 4, no. 1 (1998): article 3, http://www.fsu.edu/~trauma/art3v4i1.html (accessed November 20, 2003).

46. M. S. Gibbs, "Factors in the Victim That Mediate between Disaster and Psychopathology: A Review," *Journal of Traumatic Stress* 2, no. 4 (1989): 509.

47. B. L. Green, M. C. Grace, and G. C. Gleser, "Identifying Survivors at Risk: Long-term Impairment following the Beverly Hills Supper Club Fire," *Journal of Consulting and Clinical Psychology* 53 (1985): 672–78.

48. Carol S. North, Elizabeth M. Smith, Robert E. McCool, and Patrick E. Lightcap, "Acute Post-disaster Coping and Adjustment," *Journal of Traumatic Stress* 2, no. 3 (1989): 353–60.

49. S. Weinrich, S. B. Hardin, and M. Johnson, "Nurses Respond to Hurricane Hugo Victims' Disaster Stress," *Archives of Psychiatric Nursing* 4 (1990): 195–205.

50. D. N. Sattler, B. A. Hamby, J. M. Winkler, and C. Kaiser, "Hurricane Iniki: Psychological Functioning following Disaster (presented at the annual meeting of the American Psychological Association, Los Angeles, Ca., 1994).

51. B. W. Smith, K. I. Pargament, C. Brant, and J. M. Oliver, "Noah Revisited: Religious Coping by Church Members and the Impact of the 1993 Midwest Flood," *Journal of Community Psychology* 28, no. 2 (2000): 169–86.

52. M. Gillard and D. Paton, "Disaster Stress following a Hurricane: The Role of Religious Differences in the Fijian Islands," *Australasian Journal of Disaster and Trauma Studies* 3, no. 2 (1999), n.p.

53. K. R. Priya, "Suffering and Healing among the Survivors of Bhuj Earthquake," *Psychological Studies* 47, nos. 1–3 (2002): 106–12.

54. K. I. Pargament, K. Ishler, E. Dubow, P. Stanik, R. Rouiller, P. Crowe, E. Cullman, M. Albert, and B. J. Royster, "Methods of Religious Coping with the Gulf War: Cross-sectional and Longitudinal Analyses," *Journal for the Scientific Study of Religion* 33 (1994): 347–61.

55. K. I. Pargament, B. W. Smith, H. G. Koenig, and L. Perez, "Patterns of Positive and Negative Religious Coping with Major Life Stressors," *Journal for the Scientific Study of Religion* 37 (1998): 710–24.

56. M. A. Schuster, B. D. Stein, L. H. Jaycox, R. L. Collins, G. N. Marshall, M. N. Elliott, A. J. Zhou, D. E. Kanouse, J. L. Morrison, S. H. Berry, "A National Survey of Stress Reactions after the September 11, 2001, Terrorist Attacks," *New England Journal of Medicine* 345 (2001): 1507–12.

57. D. Biema, "Faith after the Fall," *Time Magazine*, October 8, 2001.

58. The Gallup Organization, "Poll Topics and Trends," http://www.gallup.com/poll/topics/religion.asp (accessed July 18, 2003).

59. Z. Kaplan, M. A. Matar, R. Kamin, T. Sadan, and H. Cohen, "Stress-related Responses after 3 Years of Exposure to Terror in Israel: Are Ideological-religious Factors Associated with Resilience?" *Journal of Clinical Psychiatry* 66 (2005): 1146–54.

60. H. G. Koenig, M. E. McCullough, and D. B. Larson, *Handbook of Religion and Health* (New York: Oxford University Press, 2001).

61. V. Frankel, *Man's Search for Meaning* (New York: Simon & Schuster, 1963).

Chapter 4

1. For a history of major plagues, see http://uhavax.hartford.edu/bugl/histepi.htm#plague.

2. R. Porter, *The Greatest Benefit to Mankind: A Medical History of Humanity* (New York, W. W. Norton & Company, 1997). 88.

3. C. Bradfield, M. L. Wylie, and L. G. Echterling, "After the Flood: The Response of Ministers to a Natural Disaster," *Sociological Analysis* 49 (1989): 397-407.

4. M. H. Smith, "American Religious Organizations in Disaster: A Study of Congregational Response to Disaster," *Mass Emergencies* 3 (1978): 133–42.

5. J. Veroff, R. A. Kulka, and E. Couvan, *Mental Health in America: Patterns of Help-Seeking from 1957 to 1976* (New York: Basic Books, 1981).

6. D. B. Larson, A. A. Hohmann, L. G. Kessler, K. G. Meador, J. H. Boyd, and E. McSherry, "The Couch and the Cloth: The Need for Linkage," *Hospital and Community Psychiatry* 39, no. 10 (1988): 1064–69.

7. U.S. Department of Labor, *Occupational Outlook Handbook: United States Department of Labor* (Washington, D.C.: Bureau of Labor Statistics, 1998).

8. A. J. Weaver, "Has There Been a Failure to Prepare and Support Parish-based Clergy in Their Role as Frontline Community Mental Health Workers? A Review," *Journal of Pastoral Care* 49 (1995): 129–49.

9. R. F. Mollica, F. J. Streets, J. Boscarino, and F. C. Redlich, "A Community Study of Formal Pastoral Counseling Activities of the Clergy," *American Journal of Psychiatry* 143 (1986): 323–28; from p. 323, quoted in *Counseling Survivors of Traumatic*

Events: A Handbook for Pastors and other Helping Professionals, ed. A. J. Weaver, L. T. Flannelly, and J. D. Preston (Nashville: Abingdon Press, 2003), 23.

10. D. R. Williams, E. H. Griffins, J. L. Young, C. Collins, and J. Dobson, "Structure and Provision of Services in Black Churches in New Haven, CT," *Cultural Diversity and Ethnic Minority Psychology* 5, no. 2 (1999): 118–33.

11. H. P. Chalfant, P. L. Heller, A. Roberts, D. Vriones, S. Aquirre-Hochbaum, and W. Farr, "The Clergy as a Resource for Those Encountering Psychological Distress," *Review of Religious Research* 31 (1990): 306–13.

12. L. Nelson and R. R. Dynes, "The Impact of Devotionalism and Attendance on Ordinary and Emergency Helping Behavior," *Journal for the Scientific Study of Religion* 15, no. 1 (1976): 47–59.

13. R. Chinnici, "Pastoral Care following a Natural Disaster," *Pastoral Psychology* 33, no. 4 (1985): 245–54.

14. L. G. Echterling, C. Bradfield, and M. L. Wylie, "Responses of Urban and Rural Ministers to a Natural Disaster," *Journal of Rural Community Psychology* 9, no. 1 (1988): 36–46.

15. Smith et al., "Noah Revisited: Religious Coping by Church Members and the Impact of the 1993 Midwest Flood."

16. A. J. W. Taylor, "Observations from a Cyclone Stress/Trauma Assignment in the Cook Islands," *Traumatology* 4, no. 1 (1998): article 3, http://www.fsu.edu/~trauma/art3v4i1.html (accessed November 20, 2003).

17. A. J. W. Taylor, "Value Conflict Arising from a Disaster," *Australasian Journal of Disaster and Trauma Studies* 3, no. 2 (1999), n.p., http://www.massey.ac.nz/~trauma/issues/1999-2/taylor.htm (accessed November 20, 2003).

18. Jeff Seidel, "Katrina's Aftermath: Churches Take Charge and Care for Survivors," *Detroit Free Press*, September 5, 2005 (the story appeared on Monday, one week after the hurricane hit).

19. G. Zimmerman and W. Weber, "Care for the Caregivers: A Program for Canadian Military Chaplains after Serving in NATO and United Nations Peacekeeping Missions in the 1990s," *Military Medicine* 165, no. 9 (2000): 687–90.

20. See http://umns.umc.org/02/june/262.htm.

21. See http://www.mipt.org/pdf/MIPT-OKC7-AppC-only.pdf.

22. See http://umns.umc.org/02/june/262.htm.

23. See http://www.generationxcel.com/9_11.htm.

Chapter 5

1. See http://www.adventist.communityservices.org/.

2. See http://www.nationalministries.org/abmen/news_view.cfm?subject_id=1.

3. See http://www.redcross.org/press/archives/020100.html.

4. "Volunteer Chaplains Bring Blessings to Ground Zero," 2001, http://www.redcross.org/news/ds/6month/020312chaplains.html.

5. Z. Davidowitz-Farkas, "Religious Care in Coping with Terrorism," 2004; contact zdavidowitz@mindspring.com.

6. See http://www.redcross.org/news/ds/0109wtc/020619conference.html.

7. See http://www.amurt.net/.

8. See http://www.catholiccharitiesusa.org/response/index.cfm?cfid=621566&cft oken=18055608.

9. See http://www.cdresponse.org/cdrhome.html.

10. See http://www.crwrc.org/about.html.

11. See http://www.brethren.org/genbd/ersm/disaster.htm.

12. See http://www.providentliving.org/channel/0,11677,4589-1,00.html.

13. See http://www.weekofcompassion.org/pages/about/about.html.

14. See http://www.weekofcompassion.org/pages/updates/updates.html.

15. See http://www.er-d.org/.

16. See http://www.disaster-relief.net/mavoad/mafds.html.

17. See http://www.gospelcom.net/ia/geninfo/frames/frwhoweare.htm.

18. See http://www.ldr.org/who.asp.

19. See http://www.mds.mennonite.net/pages/about.html#mission.

20. See http://www.nazarenedisasterresponse.org/.

21. See http://www.nwmedicalteams.org/who_we_are/we_are_unique.html.

22. See http://www.pcusa.org/pda/.

23. See http://rcws.rca.org/.

24. See http://www1.salvationarmy.org/.

25. See http://www.salvationarmyusa.org/WWW_USN.nsf/vw_sublinks/ 6BCE4C4AAAC85DFA80256B80003B57BB?openDocument.

26. See http://www.namb.net/dr/.

27. See http://www.ucc.org/disaster/index.html.

28. See http://www.traumaministry.org/.

29. See http://gbgm-umc.org/umcor/info.stm.

30. See http://www.dakotasumc.org/.

31. See http://www.ujc.org/aboutus_home.html.

32. See http://www.volunteersofamerica.org/xq/CFM/content_item_id.1476/ folder_id.181/qx/tier3_cd.cfm.

33. See http://www.worldvision.org/worldvision/comms.nsf/stable/ whoweare?Open.

34. See http://www.act-intl.org/act_what_is.html.

35. See http://www.aerdo.org/.

36. See http://www.cwserp.org/.

37. See http://www.cwserp.org/who.php.

38. See http://www.nvoad.org/history4.php.

39. See http://www.findflorida.org/.

40. See http://midro.missouri.org/.

41. See http://www.angelfire.com/oz/ahh/.

42. Part of Catholic Charities; see http://www.catholiccharitiesusa.org/response/ index.cfm?cfid=621566&cftoken=18055608.

43. See http://www.ncidr.org/.

44. Johanna Olson of Lutheran Disaster Relief, discussion with author, 2003.

45. Ibid.

Chapter 6

1. U.S. Department of Labor, *Occupational Outlook Handbook: United States Department of Labor* (Washington, D.C.: Bureau of Labor Statistics, 1998).

2. Princeton Religion Research Center, *Religion in America* (Princeton, N.J.: The Gallup Poll, 1996).

3. G. Piper, "People Need Help Facing Mitigation," *Disaster News Network*, October 14, 1998, http://www.disasternews.net/news/news.php?articleid=15.

4. Ibid.

5. See http://healthpolicy.stanford.edu/GHP/New%20Folder/ F&O%20presentation%20v4.pdf.

6. See http://www.disasternews.net/news/news.php?articleid=1524s

7. L. G. Echterling, C. Bradfield, and M. L. Wylie, "Responses of Urban and Rural Ministers to a Natural Disaster," *Journal of Rural Community Psychology* 9, no. 1 (1988): 39.

8. See http://www.disasternews.net/news/news.php?articleid=1821.

9. See http://www.generationxcel.com/9_11.htm.

10. H. Moyer, "DC Pastors Carry Heavy Load," *Disaster News Network*, October 11, 2001, http://www.disasternews.net/news/news.php?articleid=1297.

Chapter 7

1. Francis Gunn provided this information specifically for this report in 2003.

2. H. E. Moore, *Waco-San Angelo Disaster Study: Report on Second Year's Work* (Austin: University of Texas Press, 1958), 2.

3. See http://www.elca.org/dcs/disaster/preparetocare.pdf.

4. See http://www.elca.org/dcs/disaster/pdf/OriginalCH.pdf.

5. See http://www.elca.org/dcs/disaster/before.html.

6. This list was provided in 2003 by Lutheran Social Services of the South, Inc., and by Christine Iverson of Lutheran Social Services of Kansas and Oklahoma; see http://www.elca.org/dcs/disaster/before.html.

7. See http://www.redcross.org/static/file_cont36_lang0_23.pdf.

Chapter 8

1. A. M. Hull, D. A. Alexander, and S. Klein, "Survivors of the Piper Alpha Oil Platform Disaster: Long-Term Follow-up Study," *British Journal of Psychiatry* 181, no. 5 (2002): 433–38.

2. Johanna Olson of Lutheran Disaster Relief, discussion with author, 2003.

3. American Red Cross, *The Lifecycle of a Disaster: Ritual and Practice: Understanding the Impact of the 9/11 Terrorist Attacks on Faith Communities and Their Leaders* (New York: American Red Cross, 2002).

4. M. G. Weiss, B. Saraceno, S. Saxena, and M. van Ommeren, "Mental Health in the Aftermath of Disasters: Consensus and Controversy," *Journal of Nervous and Mental Disease* 191, no. 9 (2003): 611–15.

5. H. G. Koenig and D. B. Larson, "Religion and Mental Health: Evidence for an Association," *International Review of Psychiatry*, 13 (2001): 67–78.

6. B. D. Beitman, "Pastoral Counseling Centers: A Challenge to Community Mental Health Centers," *Hospital and Community Psychiatry* 33 (1982): 486–87.

7. Z. Davidowitz-Farkas, "Religious Care in Coping with Terrorism," 2004; contact zdavidowitz@mindspring.com

8. Zahara Davidowitz-Farkas is a rabbi and certified chaplain. She is executive director of the Institute for Disaster Spiritual Care, 150 Amsterdam Avenue, New York, NY 10163-3247 (zdavidowitz@mindspring.com or davidowitzz@arcgny.org).

9. Andrew J. Weaver, Ph.D., was research director of the HealthCare Chaplaincy in New York City (AWeaver@HealthCareChaplaincy.org).

10. A. J. Weaver, L. T. Flannelly, and J. D. Preston, *Counseling Survivors of Traumatic Events: A Handbook for Pastors and other Helping Professionals* (Nashville: Abingdon Press, 2003).

11. Rabbi Zahara Davidowitz-Farkas, discussion with author, December 30, 2003.

12. Based on e-mail correspondence, January 7, 2004.

Chapter 9

1. H. G. Koenig, *Faith and Mental Health: Religious Resources for Healing* (Philadelphia: Templeton Foundation Press, 2005).

2. See http://www.usfa.fema.gov/fire-service/grants/federal/fedguide/cfda/cfda93982.html.

3. H. G. Koenig, *The Healing Power of Faith* (New York: Simon & Schuster, 2001).

4. International Critical Incident Stress Foundation, Inc., 3290 Pine Orchard Lane, Suite 106 Ellicott City, MD 21042 (410-750-9600 or www.icisf.org).

5. Rabbi Zahara Davidowitz-Farkas, discussion with author, December 30, 2003.

6. See http://www.mipt.org/pdf/MIPT-OKC7-AppC-only.pdf.

Chapter 10: Final Comments

1. H. G. Koenig, "Volunteer," in *Purpose and Power in Retirement* (Philadelphia: Templeton Foundation Press, 2002), 71–96.

Resources

1. See http://www.fema.gov/rrr/counsel.shtm.

2. See http://www.usfa.fema.gov/fire-service/grants/federal/fedguide/cfda/cfda93982.html.

3. See http://www.mentalhealth.org/publications/allpubs/SMA03-3829/default.asp.

Glossary of Terms and Definitions

1. Many of these terms were obtained from the *Mental Health All-Hazards Disaster Planning Guide*, 2003, http://www.mentalhealth.org/publications/allpubs/SMA03-3829/default.asp.

Index